Rodney & Beverly

May God richly bless
you and your new
field of service.

Mikey & Brenda

4/18/13

PASTORING

ISN'T ALL IT'S CRACKED UP TO BE

IT'S MORE!

Roger Alford

Unless otherwise noted, all Scriptures are taken from the King James
Version. Scripture references marked NIV are taken from the New
International Version. Copyright 1973, 1978, 1984 International Bible
Society. Used by permission.

ISBN 13: 978-1481158596

Published by NCCT Publishing, PO Box 5234, Granbury, TX 76049

www.ncctpub.org

RECOMMENDATIONS

I have just finished reading "Pastoring Isn't All It's Cracked Up To Be, It's More" and found it to be enjoyable, convicting and completely on target. Having known the author, Roger Alford, for many years, I can truthfully say he has shared his life, his calling, his heart, and his soul with the readers of this book. If you are a pastor this book will bless and encourage you. If you are a layman you will find much that will speak to you and cause you to be a greater blessing to your pastor.

James Moore, Pastor Emeritus
First Baptist Church, Mansfield, TX

This book is about pastoring! There is a dearth of true pastors in the world today. I am so glad my dear friend; Pastor Roger Alford has shared some practical insights from his ministry as pastor. I believe this book will help many pastors who have a genuine calling from God to develop a more effective pastoral ministry. Pastor Roger asked a most challenging question to pastors, "Where is your glow?" This book will help you to discover, rekindle, or perpetuate the glow which comes from the glory of God in the person of Jesus Christ. And it is Christ in you which is your hope of glory!

Dr. Lewis Gregory,
Director of Source Ministries International
Snellville, GA

Roger shares not only the triumphs but also the tragedies and trials of pastoring. He is brave enough to admit that, even for God's anointed pastor, life is often unfair. Even in the midst of life's trials, you can have a life filled with joy and the peace of the Holy Spirit. Every word in this book is true, every experience real, every tear was shed and every song of laughter was sung!

Dr. Del Kennedy, Pastor
Church on the Rock, Granbury, TX

This book contains much needed explanation of the threat and dangers of legalism while admitting that decency and order are still important. It gives needed warnings why churches and denominations should avoid a "cookie cutter mentality."

L.D. Kennedy, Emeritus Professor of Literature
Campbellsville (Kentucky) University

Table of Contents

INTRODUCTION

This book is written to young pastors, pastors just starting in the ministry, and even older pastors who are starting to sag and need a "faith-lift". I have been pastoring for about 40 years, so I speak with a little experience as one who has "been there, done that". I pray that God will use this book to ENCOURAGE you. At times it may step on your toes and convict you. But I hope that by reading my story you will be inspired, instructed, and motivated.

I couldn't come up with a title that fully describes this book, so here are my sub titles:

What I didn't learn in seminary

Practical helps for pastors

Pastoring for dummies

How to give a church back to its rightful owner – Jesus

So you want a New Testament church?

Pastoring can be fun

Pastoring can be heartbreaking

Pastoring can be easy

Shortcuts to pastoring

So, you're a pastor, now what?

How not to pastor a church

The purpose of this book is to glorify God and see His Kingdom advanced. How? Through the church. Who is the church? His sheep. Sheep need a Shepherd, a pastor. The pastor needs help. God is our "ever present help". This book tells how He helped me.

I know there are a variety of denominations and independent churches, but I hope these insights can be used by all pastors. So I do not address how a local church should be governed—for example, led by one pastor, pastoral staff, elders, deacons, committee, team or congregation. Most of the instances where I use the word "man" is not intended to exclude women, but rather refers to humans. No matter what flavor your church is, this book is designed for whoever is called a "pastor," whether full-time or bi-vocational.

This book is not all inclusive. There are the many other aspects of pastoring not covered here. It is written by a human, so remember to separate the wheat from the chaff. Just don't throw out the baby with the bathwater!

I was wondering if I should publish this book. Then one day in my devotional time I came across Psalms 26:7, "That I may publish with the voice of thanksgiving, and tell of all thy wondrous works." I want to share with you some of the wondrous works that God has done in my life as a pastor.

God gets the credit and the glory for what He has taught me as a pastor and how He has used me. They are His wondrous works, not mine. I did not want to publish a book that would in any way highlight my life, so I was hesitant to publish anything that might appear to promote myself. But God convinced me through this verse that this book should declare His wondrous works. But more than just a book to help pastors, God impressed me that as pastors were helped, then their congregations could be blessed. Psalms 26:12, "In the congregations will I bless the Lord."

Now, grab yourself a cup of coffee (or a shot of wheat grass if you're a health nut), sit back, relax, and then read and enjoy.

1.

Lessons from My Early Years

God blessed me with Christian parents, and I am thankful for their influence. My mom and dad were both saved and loved the Lord Jesus. When I was seven, I realized that I was a sinner and needed a Savior. I turned from my sin and told God I was sorry for my sin. I believed that Jesus died on the cross as the payment for my sin, and I asked Him to come into my heart, forgive me, and make me His child; and at that moment I was born again.

Being raised in a Christian home, I attended church and all of its functions for my age. And I began to grow spiritually. During that time God laid many foundations in my life that I have been able to build upon and draw from ever since. However, when I hit the teenage years, I started wanting to try my own wings and developed an independent spirit. I thought I knew more than my parents knew, more than the church knew, and even more than God knew—even though I never admitted that at the time. It boils down to what is called a carnal Christian. Paul said, "I couldn't write to you as unto spiritual but as unto carnal." (I Corinthians 3:1). A carnal Christian is a Christian who is trying to live the Christian life in the energy of the flesh, rather than in the power of the Spirit. At that time I basically was trying to control my own life. In my own mind I had taken over the steering wheel. Jesus was still in my heart and life, but I had pushed Him over onto the passenger side of the car of my life, and I was trying to be in control. This didn't get me anywhere; it didn't bring me peace, joy, or fulfillment.

Something was lacking in my life: the fullness which is to be had in Christ. I had an element of that, but I wasn't walking in the Spirit. Most of the time I was walking after the flesh, not after the Spirit. I wasn't reckoning self to be dead and was not allowing Jesus to live through me like He wanted to. "Likewise, reckon ye also yourselves to be dead indeed unto sin, but alive unto God through Jesus Christ, our Lord." (Romans 6:11). However, on the outside I looked like a very nice Christian boy. I was elected president of my church youth group. I didn't do bad things; I didn't go running around partying, drinking alcoholic beverages. I didn't smoke and didn't do drugs. Outwardly I looked like an example of a fine Christian young man.

1

However, as I said, inwardly I wasn't surrendering to Jesus the controls of my life. I was making my own decisions without consulting Him (except every now and then, when I got in a pinch, I would get serious about praying and seeking His face). Things went pretty smoothly, and therefore, I didn't have to seek Him a whole lot, or I thought I didn't. I didn't have a desire to get into God's Word. But rather I spent more time reading the paper, magazines, watching TV. I wasn't feeding myself spiritually. I was still in church all right, but my mind wasn't always there. I wasn't concentrating on what was being said nor wasn't really open to what the Spirit was trying to tell me. I didn't have much of a burden for lost souls. I had my ticket to heaven. I knew I was going and really didn't care if anybody else went or not. I wouldn't admit that to myself. I would outwardly say that I cared and half way acted like that.

For instance when visitation night came along, I would feel guilty enough from the preacher preaching that we should visit, so I would show up for visitation and go out and visit and half way share the gospel with other people. But I was doing it out of guilt, duty, and obligation, not because it was coming from my heart. Therefore most of those efforts were futile, although on occasion someone might get saved as the result of me witnessing to them. But after all it is the Word of God that does the work of God. If we just unleash the Word, even Balaam's donkey can get a message across. (Numbers 22:28). But over all, there was very little success in my Christianized fleshly effort. That was a frustration in my life as well as many other frustrations. Something was lacking in my Christian life. Let me say right now, it certainly wasn't something lacking in the Lord Jesus, and it certainly wasn't His fault. He was there all the time, but I just wasn't yielding to Him.

At salvation He gave me all that is needed as II Peter 1:3 says, "According as his divine power hath given unto us all things that pertain unto life and godliness, through the knowledge of him that hath called us to glory and virtue." I just wasn't lining up my life and attitudes, nor yielding to Him to allow Him to operate in the fullness which was rightfully mine from the day I accepted Him. Part of that problem comes from Satan as a deceiver.

He comes along to lie to us and make us think there are other ways to find

2

joy, peace, and fulfillment other than yielding on a daily basis to Christ. So I fell for a big part of that lie of Satan.

I went on to college, Union University in Tennessee, and majored in Spanish because I thought that was the thing to do. I didn't particularly pray about it or seek God's face about it. It came easy to me. I thought I would be a big time interpreter for the government when I graduated. I married my high school sweetheart, Elaine, my beautiful wife of 46 years now. Thank God for His grace and mercy for giving me a wonderful spouse! While I was still in college we had a child, David. When I was about to graduate from college, our second child, Gina, was on the way.

When I graduated I lost my student deferment. This was in the midst of the Viet Nam war, so as soon as I graduated I got a letter from the President of the United States saying, "Congratulations, you have been selected to serve your country in the armed forces." I thought, "Great, this is just what I don't need. This was not in my plans; I have no desire, in fact, I don't want to go into the army." So I wrote the draft board a letter and told them I had a child and one was on the way. They wrote back saying, "Congratulations on your expected arrival, but you are still drafted." I went into the army, and I hated it. Don't take it that I hate our U.S. government. I respect our government and I pray for those who are in authority. I respect our military system and appreciate that there are people giving their lives for our freedom and others' freedom, and I am very patriotic. However, I just didn't want to be a soldier myself. I had better things to do, or so I thought. So I hated being in the army. (I repeat this for it is important for you to understand later.)

2.

Lessons from the Army

In the course of basic training I didn't appreciate the fact that here was some drill sergeant telling me what to do, how short to wear my hair, when to polish my boots, when to jump, and how high to jump. I almost despised one sergeant, who had a sixth grade education, and here I was a college graduate, and here he was with his big beer belly sticking out telling me to get down and give him ten pushups. I really didn't go for that, and I thought, "What am I doing here? I am a college graduate; this is beneath me doing this, this is not my calling in life!" So, with great resistance, however, I continued to be a good boy and I obeyed the sergeant. I realized that if you don't obey, you could get thrown in the brig and it would extend your military service time. And I wanted to be out within the two years of my draft requirement. Again, I was a good boy outwardly. I had them all fooled thinking that I was a good soldier. They advanced me five ranks in that short time (twenty two months of service). Looking back, God was trying to teach me that I had a problem with authority, and that I needed to learn to submit to authority, whether it is parents, teachers, government, or army drill sergeants. So God was teaching me some lessons. Also God had me in the army to get my attention in another way.

While I was in the army at Ft. Bragg, North Carolina, my family attended Grace Baptist Church near the base. There I met a man that God used to drastically change the course of my life. You probably never heard of him and probably never will, just a man who loved the Lord Jesus and shared his love for Jesus with me and others. His name was Don Porter. Don became a friend to me. He just didn't start preaching to me but befriended me. He and his wife, Judy, would have us in their home for meals. Don would take me out to play tennis, take me to his house to feed me, and take me on church visitation. He spent time with me and mentored me.

In everyday life, watching him deal with matters, I saw something in Don, something that I didn't have. So one day I mentioned it to him. I said, "Don, I notice that you have something I don't have; you're a Christian, I'm a Christian; you have Jesus in your heart; I have Jesus in my heart; but you seem to have a lot more peace, more joy, more fulfillment, more purpose. You obviously have a love for the Word of God, a hunger for the Word that I don't have. You obviously have a burden for lost souls. You seem to be what a Christian should be. What is it that you have that I don't have?" And the answer he gave me is important for every Christian to know. It's the secret of the happy victorious Christian life; it is the secret of how to *walk in the Spirit.* (And really it is no secret, it is right there in the Bible. I probably had it preached to me along the way, but my ears were dull of hearing and I didn't pick it up).

He began to share with me and say, "Roger," (he knew me well enough to talk to me this way) "I really believe you need to be filled with the Holy Spirit. You are so full of self there is no room for God. You can't be filled up with two things. You are full of self and selfish ways in your life rather than allowing yourself to be filled with God's Spirit." He continued to explain to me more of what all that meant. He quoted Scriptures like "I am crucified with Christ: nevertheless I live; yet not I, but Christ liveth in me; and the life which I now live in the flesh I live by the faith of the Son of God, who loved me and gave himself for me." (Gal 2:20) "Be filled with the Spirit." (Eph 5:18), "Reckon yourselves to be dead." (Romans 6:11) He urged me just to pray along those lines. So I did and prayed right then.

The best I can recall, we had just played a set of tennis, and we were just sitting on the court talking. I bowed my head right there and prayed, something to this effect, "Lord Jesus, I know I am saved. I know you are in my heart. I confess that I have been trying to control my life rather than yielding control to you. As best I know how I reckon that Roger Alford is now dead, Roger no longer lives. From now on it is not what Roger wants but what you want. Just empty me of selfish ways and fill me with your Spirit. And by your grace and as you enable me; I surrender all that I know how to surrender to you. You take control. I give you back the steering wheel of my life, and I'll sit on the passenger side." I prayed that, and God did fill me with the Spirit at that moment! I've had to reckon that and confess that quite often since. There is one baptism of the Holy Spirit and that occurs at salvation. Jesus comes in and washes away our sin, cleanses us. He fills us up from the top of our head to the bottom of our feet. However, I believe there are many fillings. Ephesians 5:18 says, "And be not drunk with wine, in which is excess, but be filled with the Spirit." Romans 8:9b says, "If anyone does not have the Spirit of Christ, he does not belong to Christ." See also Acts 2:38, Romans 6:3.

Now, when I prayed that prayer, lightning didn't flash, thunder didn't clap, I didn't have any goose bumps, I didn't have any particular feelings or emotions, I didn't cry or weep, I didn't speak in tongues, although I have nothing against any of those. At any time God can lay a certain feeling upon me or lay any particular gift of the Spirit on me, that's all up to Him. As a matter of fact, I took God at His Word; God said be filled with the Spirit, reckon yourself dead, and that's what I did. I took God at his Word, and God was faithful to His Word. Although I didn't have an immediate feeling or sensation of any kind, I began to realize that I had a whole new identity. . . in Christ! I had a hunger for the Word like I had never had before, reading, studying the Bible. I noticed myself starting to have a burden for the lost, wanting to share the good news of Jesus with others, and caring more about spiritual things. It affected all of my life; the way that I looked at my wife or my children, and including my career.

If you would like a more thorough explanation of how to better understand your identity in Christ, I suggest you read the book **Introducing The New You** by Dr. Lewis Gregory. He is my good friend and a co-laborer in the Gospel.

I was almost due to get out of the army by this stage of my life. Since the Holy Spirit was now in control of my life, I went to the Lord in prayer, and said, "Lord, what do you want me to do with my life? Should I be a Spanish interpreter, banker, lawyer, ditch digger, whatever? I am willing to enter any occupation now that I am about to get out of the army. What do you want me to enter into?" I got no immediate answer. I continued to pray and seek the Lord for that answer, (sometimes that is not so bad—it's not a bad position to be on your knees!) And He kept me on my knees for a while, seeking Him.

As my time was approaching very close to getting out of the army, I was praying one day coming home from work on the base. I said, "God, I really would like you to tell me." And God said to my heart, "Have you surrendered everything to me?" I said, "Yes, Lord, I believe I have surrendered everything to you. I don't know of any reason why you haven't answered my prayer on wanting direction." God basically said, "I want you to re-enlist in the army." I thought, "Oh no, anything but that, God, oh no, Lord. What I hate to do worst in life.

I hate being in the army; surely, not that!

Roger Alford is dead and that is not what Roger wants, but if that is what <u>you</u> want, then tomorrow when I get back to base I will go into the enlistment office, and I will re-enlist. If you want me to make a career out of the army, fine." Then God said, "No I didn't want you to re-enlist. I just wanted that last area of your life that you hadn't surrendered to me. Now you have surrendered this thing of staying in the army, now that you have completely surrendered, I will tell you what I want you to do. I don't want you to stay in the army. . . . . I want you to preach. I want you to be a preacher." Well, I thought maybe I wasn't hearing from God on that one! Maybe I was hearing some other voice, because I had a miserable time in high school speech class. I was not a public speaker, I got really nervous. I let the Lord know this, I was arguing with the Lord on the way home. "I can hardly get in front of a crowd without my knees knocking and my voice shaking and my throat going dry; God, I just can't. Are you sure God?" He reminded me of Moses, "I made your mouth and if I call you to do something I will give you what it takes to do it." (Exodus 4:11-12) I said, "OK Lord."

I began to weep tears of joy that God had finally told me what He wanted me to do with my life. He gave me this new direction in my life, and then I began crying even more when I realized that of all the people He could have chosen, He chose <u>me</u> to be a preacher for Him. So I was just bawling as I was driving. I guess my guardian angel kept that car on the road because I surely couldn't see the road. I got home and my wife met me at the front door, as was her custom. She asked me why I was crying. I blurted out, "God just now called me to preach." And she said, "That doesn't surprise me." Again, I thank God for a wonderful wife. Even though she didn't marry a preacher, she was fully behind me and fully supported me and has fully supported me ever since, and I thank God for her and her attitude.

A few days later I went and shared with my pastor, Dwight Cooper, what God had done in my life and that He had called me to preach. He praised the Lord with me and told me I was to preach the next Sunday morning (I did and I was not even nervous).

On one Sunday morning I got up and started dressing for church. My wife and I shared one dresser in our small bedroom. The top of the dresser was a catch all and I always emptied my pants pockets and put my change, keys, comb, pocket knife, and hanky on top of the dresser. So, I put all those items in my dress pants, and we hurried off to church. We sat on the front pew. I had a cold and my nose started to run. I reached into my pocket and pulled out my hanky to blow my nose. I had a habit of shaking open my hanky, and when I did I saw it was not a hanky but a pair of my wife's panties! In my haste to get dressed, I had grabbed the wrong item from our dresser. In a flash I crammed the panties back into my pocket. I just sniffed for the rest of the service! Pastor, always check your attire before leaving the house. Check your zipper also!

Pastor Cooper said to me, "Where are you going to go to seminary?" "Well," I said, "I don't plan on going to seminary. I finally got to that place where I know it's nothing of the flesh, it's nothing of man, it has to be the Holy Spirit. The Holy Spirit lives in me and has filled me, and by His power I can go preach and be a preacher, and I don't need anything man has to offer." He said he heard what I was saying, but sometimes God leads us to get further training, education, to sharpen ourselves, to sharpen our calling. etc. "That is not for me, I don't need it." And he said, "Roger would you at least pray about whether you should go to seminary?" "Oh yes, I will pray about it, that won't hurt anything."

As I started praying about it, I didn't feel any particular inclination one way or another because I had come across some great, dynamic, Spirit filled preachers who could really preach the Word of God in power. One particular pastor that I had didn't have a seminary education. James Moore knew how to preach with Holy Ghost power. Sometimes when he preached, it seemed as though his eyes would glow, smoke would come out of his ears, fire would shoot from his nostrils, and the sharp sword of the Word of God would come out of his mouth and penetrate the hardest heart!

I thought if he doesn't need seminary, I don't need it. I also had, on occasion, heard preachers who had some long degrees behind their name—formal education. And some of those that I heard were dry and boring. I thought, "If that is what seminary does to you, I don't want it." However, I continued to pray about it and the Lord impressed upon me that I needed to go to seminary. Not that He sends all men. He assured me of that, and it wasn't that I had to go. He wanted me to go. So I pursued that.

I was due to get out of the army in October. This was about the first of July. To get out of the army in time to go to seminary by the first of September, I would need what they call an "early out." They allow you to get out a little early if that is what it takes for you to go on and start some type of school. So, I applied for an "early out" and got that paper work started. They are not obligated to give you an "early out." In order to get an "early out," part of the process requires a physical. To get into the army you get a physical; to get out of the army you also have to get a physical. I guess, so that if you have some type of health problem later on you can't blame the military service for that.

So I called over to the hospital on base and told them I needed an "early out" physical. They let me know that I wasn't scheduled to get my physical until October, and they had a long waiting list of physicals; there was no way, and they had no time to work me in front of everybody else. I would just have to wait my turn and basically forget about it. I thought, "OK." So I went back to the Lord and said, "You have a problem. You are the one who told me I was supposed to go get a physical, get out of here, and go to seminary. Seminary starts the first of September, however, they told me that I can't get a physical. So, Lord, this is your problem and I am not worried about it. Roger Alford is dead, and I will just leave it in your hands." So I figured that if He wants me in seminary in September He would take care of it. If I didn't get the physical, I am supposed to do something else.

One day, shortly after that, I was on my way to work at base and there was a fellow hitchhiking. He was a soldier in uniform and normally I am not in the habit of picking up hitchhikers. My Momma told me that if you pick up hitchhikers, they will knock you in the head and rob you. But something impressed me (actually someone impressed me, the Spirit of God). He told me to pull over and give this guy a ride; so I did. He got in the car and said, "Man, thank you for giving me a ride. I couldn't get my car started, and I was hoping that someone would pick me up as I am hitchhiking to base to work. You really did me a big favor." He said, "If there is any favor I could ever do for you, let me know." I said, "The only thing I need is an "early out" physical." He said, "I happen to be the non-commissioned officer in charge of giving "early out" physicals. You come by in the morning at 8 o'clock and come straight in the door. Don't worry with the line and come straight to me." I said, "Hallelujah!" The

9

next morning I went straight in the door and walked past a long line, and he ran me through first thing and gave me the early out physical!

Well there was another little glitch that had to be taken care of. (Although it appeared to be a problem, it was really just an opportunity for God to work.) By this time I had made the rank of E4, however, you had to be an E5 for the army to move you. I wasn't making a lot of money being the low rank that I was. We just lived from hand to mouth each day, and I certainly didn't have the money to move my family and my furniture to Texas where I had enrolled at Southwestern Baptist Theological Seminary. I put that one before the Lord. My immediate officer in charge over me had put in the paperwork for me to advance to another rank. Of course that is quite a deal as there have to be slots open for that rank, you have to go through an interview process, and that can take a lot of time. I thought, "Well, Lord, I am leaving this in your hands." In record time I was called in for an interview, was given the added rank, promoted to E5, which meant that the army was obligated to actually pay for my move, come in and pack me up, bag and baggage, all of my furniture, and move me, free of charge, hallelujah! So God took care of that also. By this time, it was confirmed to me that I am walking in God's will. So we moved to Texas, went through Seminary and graduated from there in three and one half years.

3.

Lessons from Seminary Days

Remember that seminary came after my stint in the army. God knew what He was doing. Because I had been in the army, I qualified for the GI Bill. I received a check for over $400 every month from Uncle Sam which really helped us while I was in seminary. And the church we attended while in the army paid my seminary tuition! God didn't have me in the army for nothing. There are a multitude of reasons He does what He does in our lives. Sometimes you see it and sometimes you don't. But it became very evident to me. I thank the Lord that He financed our way through seminary, even my little part time job.

God taught me a lot during my time at seminary. I realized what God had been trying to tell me through the counsel of my pastor that I needed to go to seminary. It wasn't so much the material that I learned while I was in seminary; you can do that in self-study. I had the privilege of sitting under the teaching of some godly men. I heard a saying once, "If you want to be a spiritual giant you have to hang around spiritual giants." So, by being on campus at seminary and sitting in on the classes, I got to hang around spiritual giants. I got to learn and hear from some of these godly professors firsthand about how to walk with God, and about the principles of Scripture.

I was also exposed to many other things in seminary, other great brothers in Christ and men who had been "called." I learned of resources, ministries, missionaries, ideas, new methods. So I became more broadminded and less legalistic. I began to realize that although there was only one true Gospel, there could be a variety of methods and personality styles to present it. See I Corinthians 1:10-13. Jesus told His disciples that if men were not against Him, they were for Him. See Mark 8:38-40.

I got involved with a fantastic church in seminary where God taught me some valuable lessons. We had a pastor there, named Bill Warren of Southwayside Baptist Church in Ft. Worth, TX. As I mentioned earlier, I had sat under some great, dynamic preaching by a former pastor. But in Bill Warren, I saw a pastor's heart.

I learned by walking with this man, being around this man, and rubbing shoulders with this spiritual giant what it meant to pastor, what it meant to love and shepherd the flock. This man just oozed with the love of Jesus. So I thank God for the privilege of getting to walk with him for a little time in my life.

Also, while in this church there were many opportunities to serve the Lord. Some preacher boys would say, " I am going to start serving the Lord when I graduate from seminary. I will wait until I get that big church out there somewhere, then I will start serving God." But God impressed upon me that what I needed to do was serve Him wherever there was opportunity and not wait for some degree and not wait for some church that I could pastor. Opportunities came up through this church. They had a jail ministry, a rescue mission ministry, a ministry to go out and visit people to share Christ with them, a nursing home ministry. So I went and preached at those places.

I got to put into practice some of the things that I was learning. I didn't have to wait for some big event. I would go out on weekly visitation with our church there. It made sense to me that if I was going to end up in a church some day and be asking people to serve in the church, but if I wasn't willing to do it myself now, who was I to expect others to serve the Lord through the various ministries of my future church? My wife and I sang in the choir, helped in the nursery and got totally involved in the life of that church.

After a while, God called me to pastor my first church in Tanglewood, Texas, three hours away from the seminary. You have to realize that because there were hundreds of seminary students it was hard to find open churches that were close to the seminary. So I thank God that this little church called me to be their part-time pastor. They were in the habit of calling seminary students. I am very thankful they were very patient with me. As I look back on some of those early sermons that I preached, a lot of them were probably pretty shallow. Not that I was preaching untruth, but I had a long way to go in God growing me in my preaching and pastoring skills.

The members were good to us and I thank God for Tanglewood Baptist Church, a little wide spot in the road. They paid me $50.00 a week which basically covered expenses to get there and back. But they did have a furnished parsonage. Every weekend we loaded the car with our luggage and two small children, and drove to Tanglewood. I would do some visitation on Saturday, and mix and mingle with the folks. I preached in the morning and evening services on Sunday.

Then we came back home after church on Sunday night, or sometimes on Monday morning. (There weren't any seminary classes on Monday, which allowed preachers like myself to be away on the weekend.) I also had another part-time job on Mondays and after class during the week. I worked at a place that sold packaging material to the meat industry, including automatic chicken baggers!

I remember a couple of humorous things that happened at Tanglewood. I led the singing one Sunday and asked if anyone in the congregation had any requests for a hymn we could sing. Troy, a little boy about four years old, shouted out, "Kiss an Angel Good Morning." You don't recognize that hymn? That's because it wasn't a hymn but a popular country and western song by Charlie Pride! The congregation broke out into laughter, and I learned to be more careful about asking for audience participation!

For a revival meeting we had a musician, Leigh Rocke, a converted night club entertainer. As I was introducing him before he got up to sing, I said, "Leigh and I have a strange and wonderful relationship. He is strange and I am wonderful." But, Pastor, remember that the next speaker after you has the microphone. Leigh got up and said, "I thought about saying something about Roger, but there's no need to set fire to a sinking ship!"

After about a year, God said He was through with me there at that church. I didn't understand why because I hadn't finished seminary yet. Usually a preacher doesn't leave one church unless he has another one lined up. That wasn't the case with me. God made it very clear to me that I was to resign. So we started attending church again where we had before, Southwayside.

I still had the fall semester to go and I was to graduate in December. In the spring before that I had been contacted by the Dean of Men, Trozy Barker, at the seminary. He told me that he had heard of a church in Kansas that was looking for a pastor to at least, if nothing else, serve for the summer. Well, I already had plans with this job that I had to work full-time for the summer.   However, I didn't want to shut this door. I wanted to make sure that God was still able to lead me anyway He wanted to. I asked him where this church was. He said, "It is in southwest Kansas, close to Dodge City, a town called Hanston." I talked it over with my wife, and we both thought, "Kansas?" We had never been in the state and all we knew about Kansas was "The Wizard of Oz." I told him we were not interested. The Lord has a way that He makes His will known to us, and although I wasn't interested, God was.

A few weeks had gone by and Trozy approached me again and said, "I really think you are the man for the job; they really want someone to come up and preach. I encourage you to go and talk with them about it." I asked him who the contact there was. He said the contact was a man who knew a missionary he (the dean) personally knew. This missionary had been serving in Viet Nam, and when the war got over the missionary had been sent home. While this missionary was in Viet Nam he knew an Air Force helicopter pilot who would fly this missionary around to some of his preaching points when he had some spare time. This pilot got out of the Air Force and was a member of the church in Hanston, Kansas which was looking for a pastor.

So he contacted his missionary friend who lived close to the seminary and thought he might know someone to send up, who in turn contacted the Dean of men, and the Dean contacted me. The Dean of Men said it this way, "Go up for the weekend; preach to the people. They will feed you and put you up. Look at it like a mini-vacation; at least give it a try." I said, "OK," and we went up one weekend to Hanston, a thriving metropolis of three hundred people, a farming community in the middle of the wheat fields of western Kansas. We got to meet the people, they fed us, and we stayed in their homes.

My wife and I had already figured out what our budget would need for the summer. I knew that it was going to take $200 a week. That is what I would have made at the summer job where I had been working in Ft. Worth, but I wasn't about to tell that to that church. I have made it a general rule in my ministry to never make my financial needs known to anyone but God. "God I want to know if you are in this, and I'm going to leave that to You for confirmation." Things went well. Our host family grilled us a big, thick, juicy, delicious, Kansas corn fed beef steak that hung off both sides of the plate. I ate that and thought it was wonderful and I could almost feel the call to come here and pastor He fed me another one and another—I ate three of those steaks in one sitting! It was fantastic—of course we didn't want that to influence our decision—did I? You see, one of my favorite Bible verses is when God told Peter in Acts 10:13 to "Rise and eat!" Besides, coming out of the army, we were poverty stricken and being in seminary we certainly couldn't afford steak.

So by the time I had finished preaching on Sunday night, the church's pulpit committee said to me, "We've already talked to you quite a bit and interviewed you about coming here and being our pastor this summer. We are going to go back in the room and talk about your salary, so, if you don't mind sit out here with your family." In a little bit they came back out and said, "We talked and prayed about it. Our last pastor was here full time and he had five children, and we paid him $135 a week. We are going to step out on faith. We want to make an offer now." Do you want to guess how much they offered me? Remember earlier I said that to stay in Ft. Worth I needed $200 a week? Well, you guessed it $200 a week! "Now," they said, "We can't promise you we can pay that, we are stepping out on faith. If you are the man for the job, God will bless your ministry and our church, and the money will come in to support you." That was further confirmation, but still I said I would go home and pray about it.

On the way home driving back to Ft. Worth the next day, Elaine and I talked about it, and she said, "You know, Rog, you need to watch out for your family, and you know they have a lot of tornadoes." I said, "Honey, that's right. I do need to watch out for my family." And it is true we don't need to go out and presume upon God; and God gave me my family long before he gave me a call to preach. I believe (in order of priority) my relationship with God comes first, my second priority is my wife and ministering to her needs, after that my children, and third comes the ministry that God puts me in. Lo and behold, when we pulled into Ft. Worth that evening and stopped at the shopping center, we heard sirens going off all over. We asked one of the workers at the store what were those sirens—we had never heard them before. The worker said, "Well, those are tornado sirens." That very evening three tornadoes touched down in Ft. Worth, Texas! So needless to say, my wife and I looked at each other and said, "I think God wants us to go to Kansas!"

So we called the church and told them we were coming. We spent the summer there and had a glorious time pastoring them. The church grew

15

mightily by the grace of God. They were running thirty people when I got there—by the end of the summer we were running about one hundred people. It had tripled in size. I just thank God. Many souls were saved, lives touched, marriages healed, and Christians renewed.

Then it came time for me to go back for the fall semester—my last one to finish up in seminary. The church asked me if I would consider staying on as their pastor. I told them, "God called me to seminary and He wants me to finish and get my degree." They said, "Well, how about if we would fly you back and forth on the weekend?" We prayed about that, and the Lord confirmed that it would be fine. We moved back to Ft. Worth for the fall semester, but every weekend my wife would drive me to the Dallas-Ft. Worth Airport, and I would catch a plane and fly into Liberal, Kansas. One of the church members, a widow, loaned me a car to drive back and forth from Liberal to Hanston. The people in the church would put me up in their homes, and I got to visit and get to know the people as well as minister on Sundays. That happened all semester. Guys would stop me in the hallway at seminary and ask me, "Are you the one that flies to Kansas every weekend to pastor?"

4.

Lessons from My First Full-Time Church

Following graduation from seminary we moved onto the church field in Hanston to become their full time pastor. I was there about two years. Things were going great, people were being saved just about every week—all ages; children, youth, adults; it was glorious. I learned a little lesson, when God works in great ways like that, the devil gets very upset. In fact, it makes the devil mad, and he starts throwing whatever he can throw and using whatever he can use. After a while the honeymoon was over with the church. A few people didn't care for the thrust of my ministry. Basically, there were some man-made traditions of the church that were getting in the way of the church's progress. I was preaching in such a way to have those traditions removed so God could move more in the ways He wanted to. But God's ways are not always man's ways. There were a group of people in the church who didn't go along with that, so they started their campaign to stop progress. I don't think they really wanted to stop growth, they just wanted growth on their terms. They didn't understand and they thought they were saving their church, but they were only saving their traditions. (I will cover more of this concept later in the book).

We had some pretty tough stuff going on there. They started doubting that I was hearing from God and basically told me I was wrong and so was the approach I was taking. I started questioning if God had really called me there. "Did you really call me to preach? It looks like it's getting to be a mess; God, are you in all of this?" But as usually the case, our trials only come to make us strong. So this drove me to my knees and deeper into the Word. I had to reexamine my theology, my understanding of church, my understanding of the role of pastor. I gleaned from the Word of God's confirmation. "In the multitude of counselors there is safety." (Proverbs 11:14). I called some godly people that The Lord had put into my life. I made some out-of-state phone calls and got counsel from men whom I considered my pastors. Their counsel was, if God called you to be the pastor, you are the shepherd of that church. You continue to lead. You can't give in to the whims of the people. Even though they may disagree with you, if God is leading a certain direction, you have to lead them in that direction. You must take a stand, and be willing to die.

17

It had come to the point that I had to be willing to put career on the line, realizing that I had rather obey God and lose my job, obey God and lose my reputation, obey God and lose my future career. I could be canned and fired from the church or whatever. I knew that I could bend, and I could compromise my conviction. Nothing wrong with bending; I believe you ought to bend over backwards to accommodate people except to the point you have to compromise your convictions. I had some definite convictions on how God was leading me to pastor. So I wasn't about to compromise that. Basically, it was just a fresh opportunity to grow in another area in my life: to give the church to the Lord, give the whole situation to God and realize it was God's church. It wasn't my church; these were God's people. These were God's sheep; they weren't mine. Again, it was His problem, an opportunity to do whatever He said do.

It got worse as far as the verbal attack on me and the way I was pastoring and preaching. The deacons would usually meet with me after Sunday School and before the worship service started on Sunday morning to pray with me in my office. On one occasion they met with me to pray and instead of uplifting me in prayer, they started laying down the law to me telling me what to preach, what not to preach. I had recently been preaching a series on the theme of love. I had discovered that many years ago some grudges had come up amongst some families in the church. I realized that we could go no further than where we were unless we learned to operate in love, and unless we learned to forgive one another of past grudges, and be willing to lay down the hatchet.

So I was preaching on love every Sunday morning from a different angle and from a different text. God had lain upon me that until they started walking in love with one another, our church was not going to do much more. I was preaching on that and hitting it every Sunday, and the deacons told me this one Sunday: "We are tired of hearing all this preaching on love. We want you to get off that and onto some other subject. If we want to hold grudges, that is our business, so get beyond that and preach on something else." So with those wounds still fresh in me, and with those words rambling around in my brain, somehow I managed, by God's grace, to pull myself up into the pulpit and I preached on . . . . love. I was not about to yield to man's opinion!

18

Quite frankly, I didn't care if the deacons and every person in the church told me they didn't like hearing that. That is what God had laid on my heart to preach and that is what I preached. I preached it again, and of course that was throwing salt into the wound as far as some were concerned. Things continued to worsen. Criticism, negativism, backbiting, gossiping, and slandering just continued to get worse. People began to take sides. I continued to try to walk with my head held high and my eye on the goal, but it was very difficult to do so. Difficult in my flesh of course: my mind, will, and emotions, even my soul. Christ said, "My yoke is easy, and my burden is light." (Matthew 11:30) In my spirit man it was not difficult. His yoke is easy. But I had to really get before Him in the prayer closet, and dig through Scriptures.

One day I will never forget, I was sitting in my office just looking for some answers in the Bible and happened to be reading about Jesus' crucifixion, the mock trial, the scourging that He took, the beating, the verbal abuse, the crucifixion itself. As I read that, I realized, "Jesus, you have been down this road before, and you have suffered many, many times more than I am suffering here. But Jesus, thank you, that you are allowing me to have a little taste of the suffering you went through: how all your friends forsook you, how Judas betrayed you, and how you must have felt at that time and some of the agony that you went through going to the cross. Lord, thank you; you did that for me, and I am getting a little taste of it."

I realized it was my sins that put Him on that cross. So with that new appreciation and from that strength, I realized that same Jesus lived within me, and He knew how to take that kind of stuff. Again, reckoning myself dead, it didn't matter what they said about Roger Alford, it didn't really matter. I don't deny reality; yes, it was hurting. But the reality was my life was hidden with Christ in God, and God was working all things for my good, and God is on the throne. I just kept on. However, the situation in the church did not improve. No matter how much I talked or shared or pleaded for us to learn to walk together in love, they were determined not to. I didn't really feel led to press it for a vote. That could have really caused a really big stink that I just didn't feel led to get into. I had not been there long enough to gain the confidence of the church as a whole. So I was asking God to move me to another church, because obviously

19

there I had led them as far as I could lead them, as far as they wanted to go. It was like hitting a brick wall on the issues of love, tradition, and denominationalism.

The devil doesn't care what the issue is. Quite frankly, he wants to destroy the church and the church's witness. That is exactly what he was doing, and I believe that he was sitting back in a corner laughing. Many people in the church had gotten their eyes off of Jesus and put them on issues that really weren't issues and got on a high horse about some things. They made a major case out of things that weren't major, more concerned about who they could run down rather that going to win a soul for Jesus, or ministering to a poor person, or ministering to someone that is down and out.

One thing I have learned over the years of pastoring is that people in a church that are not actively involved in the lives of other people and ministering to them are the very people who, when the opportunity presents itself by Satan, will be duped by him into making a mountain out of a mole hill. It might be going off on tangents becoming very negative people, griping, complaining, murmuring just like the children of Israel in the wilderness; throwing cold water on any type of progress; resisting the movement of the Spirit of God in their own lives and in the life of the church. It's quite a truth—quite a principle, an observation that God gave me early in my ministry.

I am glad that early in my ministry I learned that, hey, people are people, and even some people who seem to be pillars in the church, who maybe have a lot of positions in the church, can get sidetracked by Satan. Although some of them involved thought it was Satan, others thought it was their own opinion, their own ideas. Some thought perhaps if I resigned and left that church, that the problems would be over, and the church would get back like it used to be. (Well, yes, it got back to where it used to be, all right. We had been running thirty when I started, and they got back to running about thirty after I left.) There came a point where I was calling around saying, "Does anybody out there know where there is a church I might pastor? I want out of this one!" There is a time to stay and a time to go. Like the song that goes, "you got to know when to hold 'em, and know when to fold 'em, know when to walk away, know when to run." Sometimes I've stayed; sometimes I have gone. In this particular case God told me to leave this church. But I didn't have any place to go. There was no church out there talking to me about becoming their pastor. Finally, it was on a Wednesday night at prayer meeting. We were praying, and all of a sudden God said, "Now is the time." So, in my prayer, I resigned my position as pastor. My wife was even surprised. She knew I had been thinking about it, but the timing was quite a shock to her as well as others. Frankly, some of the people who had been adversarial to me really didn't want to see me leave—they just wanted me to change my approach. So I think it surprised many, but be that as it may, God gave me the liberty and direction to resign. I didn't have a place to go. I gave a month's notice.

It was getting to the end of that month and I told the Lord, "I don't have a place to preach. What do you want me to do once I am through here?" And He said, "I called you to Southwestern Kansas to preach the gospel, and I still want you to be here preaching the gospel. Even though you don't have a building to preach in after your time is up here, if I want you to preach on the street corners, what is that to you? You just be willing." I said, "Yes, Lord. What about my family, for Lord, you know we are living in the parsonage, and we are going to have to get out, so where are we supposed to live?" And the Lord impressed upon me, "If I want you to put your clothes in a suitcase, and put your suitcase in the trunk of your car and live out of it, what is that to you? You be willing." And I said, "Yes, Lord, I am willing to do that." As you can see, that was no specific direction—God was just telling me not to worry about it. "You just keep on keeping on and I will take care of you."

Again, my dear wife, I thank God for her, wasn't worried, even though she was expecting our third child, Joel. She did ask me these questions I had asked God, and I told her what the Lord had shared with me, and so that satisfied her, and she began packing without knowing where we were going. We had all the boxes and suitcases packed sitting on the floor the day before we were to get out of the parsonage with no idea about the next step. Talking about where to live, you have to realize that out there in that little Kansas town there were no apartments you could move into. They didn't have rental houses readily available. Most people lived in the house that they had always lived in and that was it. Most of them were farmers so it wasn't like in a metropolitan area, but there we were.

Two of the church members stopped by to visit the day before we were to move out. They were very supportive of me this whole time (and, like me were willing for the church to progress and go on beyond some of the dead traditions.) They asked, "What are you going to do, and where are you going to go?" I shared with them what God had told me: "I am supposed to preach here in southwestern Kansas, so, I guess I will preach on the street corner." "Where are you going to live?" And I said God told me that I should be willing to live out of my suitcases. And they said, "Well, if you need a place to live, we have a vacant farmhouse in the country on one of our farms. Your family is welcome to go out there and live in that home. Just play like it is yours and live there at no charge. It would be good for you, and it would be good for the house to keep it from deteriorating and running down. I said, "Thank you, brothers, and I will take you up on that. We will move out there tomorrow."

And then they asked, "What are you going to do when Sunday rolls around, where will you be preaching?" And I said, "Well, I guess I will be preaching in the living room of that house to my wife and kids." They said they would be there with their families, and I said, "Praise the Lord, brothers!" The word got out as they started sharing that we would be living at the farmhouse out in the country in the middle of a wheat field, and that I would preach that following Sunday morning.

5

Lessons from Our House Church

Sunday morning, I looked out the living room window, and it looked like a parade of cars coming down our driveway! There were a few families that left the same church I had pastored but I don't think I would call it a church split. These were the families that were sick and tired of the situation that I had described. They thought that God was through with them in that church. They felt like they were being suppressed in their vision that God had given them. They felt ousted from the church; they felt as if they had been cut off from the church.

Some people came from the Methodist church in the nearby town of Burdett. Some of these people had been coming over on Sunday nights to the Hanston church and getting fed. They didn't like some of the liberal tendencies in the particular church they were in. (Their pastor at that time did not believe in the infallibility of the Scriptures, Adam and Eve weren't literal people, and taught that Revelation was a myth!) They said they had been waiting for something like this—a new work to start. Some people came that weren't going to church anywhere. They said they hadn't been going anywhere because they didn't know of any church around where they fit in and where God was moving. They felt like this was a great opportunity for this to happen.

We started out with about forty people that Sunday morning, filling our living and dining rooms. One of the ladies played the piano. We sang some songs and I preached. We didn't pass an offering plate (there wasn't anything to pass one for). Some people said, "I have some money to give, and you are going to need money to live," so they stuck it in my hand or pocket. Would you believe that by the time they all went out the door what was given to me was within $20 of what I would have made of my salary at the previous church. (By the way, that week I got a check in the mail for. . . you guessed it—$20!). Then every week, after that, people would give varying amounts anywhere between $50 - $1,000. I never knew from one week to the next what I would be making as far as income.

I learned just to leave that in God's hands and trust Him to supply all of my needs according to His riches in glory. (Philippians 4:19) I believe that I was doing His will. God finances His programs, which He did since

I was in His program! It was not something I selected to do, but I was led by God. I learned that when I am doing what God wants me to do, He supplies the funds. Sometimes God would provide side jobs (tent making) for me. One time when I was helping a farmer shovel hog manure, he said, "I bet they didn't teach you this in seminary!" He was right, but I had learned in life, a good work ethic from my Dad and not to expect handouts.

Sometimes a pastor may be in a small church that can't fully fund him, or even a larger church may sometimes get in a financial pinch. It never hurts any preacher to get his hands dirty. Sometimes, I'd help ranchers fix fences. One rancher asked me if I had a P.H.D. degree. I said, "No, but I do know how to use a Post Hole Digger!" On occasion I helped a member run his trash route and picked up garbage. I roofed a house. Don't make your family starve because you are too "spiritual" to work. God is your source—not the church. However, if a church does not pay the pastor when they are able, they are missing out on God's blessing. (Philippians 4:17).

Sometimes God's provision came by way of money, sometimes it came in the way of meat. They would keep our freezer full of beef and pork. I remember one lady who called and said, "Pastor, I would love to give you a love offering to help you. I appreciate your ministry, but I don't have much cash. I raise chickens, so could I give you some of them?" "Absolutely!" This reminds me of a joke: What is another name for a preacher's stomach? – A graveyard for dead chickens. The next Saturday we went over to her house and helped her kill and pluck fifty chickens. We took them home and put them in our freezer, and boy, were they good.

Sometimes I would be out visiting our members, and most of them had gas barrels on their farm. They would say, "Before you leave, pull your car over and fill up with gas." Sometimes they would buy specific things for us. One of them bought an air conditioner and put it in our window. God taught me that He could supply our needs, even though we didn't have the cash.

One day a church member, named Gordon, called to see if I had time to go to Dodge City with him on an errand. I said I could (I always cherished one-on-one time with brothers like him). We pulled into a men's store and he said, "God impressed me to buy you a full set of clothes." So I got a new sports coat, pants, shirt, tie, socks, shoes— the works! Friend, you don't need a big paycheck— just a big God! One time we were about to leave on a long trip to see our relatives when a member noticed my tires were bald. He bought me four new tires! God is good. One lady asked my wife what size clothes my daughter wore. In a couple of days she came by and surprised Gina with a new dress!

Another time my wife needed surgery. The hospital asked if I had insurance. We didn't because we couldn't afford the premiums. So the hospital informed me that I could return at 6:00 PM to pick up my wife and I'd better have $600 cash to pay the bill. During the day I went about my normal pastoral duties. I visited in the home of one of our members, Ross. I did not let him know of my financial need. On the way out the door, he put a check in my hand. When I got in the car, I looked at it. Would you like to guess how much it was? Exactly $600! Our God is able! One Christmas it was going to be pretty slim for our kids. Out of the blue, Elaine's brother, George, sent the children an Atari (one of the original video game players). One family blessed my wife with a new set of expensive pots and pans.

We had an old car that had many miles on it and was totally worn out. It burned a quart of oil every forty miles and blew ugly smoke out the tailpipe. We were praying and asking God for a better car. Elaine was specifically asking for a station wagon (for those long trips to grandparents, with kids and luggage). One dark night we were returning to our home. All of a sudden in front of me appeared three black cows crossing the road. I hit the brakes and swerved, but I hit a cow. That totaled our car, and it totaled the cow. Thankfully, we were OK. But now we had no car at all. A couple days later, I got a long distance call from Oklahoma. The caller was related to one of the families in our church. He said, "Roger, I heard that you wrecked your car. Have you bought another car yet?" I said that I had not (and chuckled to myself, "with what?") He said, "I have a car that I was going to trade in on a new one, but I would like to give it to you. It's an Oldsmobile, low mileage, and in excellent condition, but you may not want it because it is a . . . . (ready for this?) station wagon." I said, "That's exactly what my wife has been praying for. You are an answer to prayer." Friend, if God takes care of the birds of the air, and the lilies of the field, He will even more so take care of you! (Matthew 6:25-34).

Another time, I was on the way to visit a family in our church. I knew I was running low on gas and I didn't have money to buy any. But I knew God wanted me to visit this family. So I headed out. About halfway there, I ran out of gas. I walked to a nearby farmhouse to call them and let them know I wasn't going to be able to make the visit. In just a few minutes here he comes with a can of gas. He told me to come on over to his house for the visit. After the visit, he filled my tank from his gas barrel!

Dear pastor, we walk by faith. So, start walking (or driving) and along the way God will provide. Hebrews 11:8 says, "By faith Abraham, when he was called to go out into a place which he should after receive for an inheritance, obeyed; and he went out, not knowing where he went."

I wasn't making a big salary—the most love offerings I ever received in a year were $15,000—and that was gross, out of that came my expenses! I do remember praying, "Lord, as my children get older, they may desire to go to college. And certainly on my income there is no way I could afford to send them." The Lord told me not to worry about it, so I didn't. I just left that to the Lord and went about my business. (More on this issue later).

Another example of God's provision for our family was when our daughter, Gina, was about to have a birthday. Birthdays were a big deal in our family. But I had no money to buy her a present. I complained to God, "I don't mind if I myself have to live in poverty, but, Lord, it's not fair that my daughter has to do without!" The morning of her birthday, I went to the mailbox, and there was a letter from some law firm in Texas. I opened it, and it said that the estate of my former boss (whom I had worked for in seminary) had been settled and he left me $2,000 in his will! I showed the check to the family, and we all rejoiced and thanked God for His mercy. Boy, did we ever celebrate Gina's birthday! God is always on time.

It was a great lesson learned there while we were in that church in our home, walking by faith and trusting the Lord to supply our needs, rather than looking to a paycheck or looking to man. I will always value those lessons. Every now and then I have to be reminded of that because ever since then I have been in churches where I received a salary. And it is easy to be tempted to revert back to thinking like the old man thinks. For example being concerned about where the money is going to come from, or how the bills are going to get paid. So, I just praise the Lord for that whole experience.

I remember after I had been there a while some of the people in the church that I had left refused to speak to me or wave at me when I would drive down the road, because they were angry with me for staying in the community. Some of them said, "If you had left, it would have been different, but you stayed in our community, and I don't know why." It shouldn't have made any difference to them, because the only people that came out of their church were the people they were disgruntled against anyhow, so you'd think I would have done them a favor. And concerning the other people that had not been going to church anywhere, you'd think they would have been glad about that. It was difficult going into the grocery store, service station, post office, running into people who ignored you. Again the Lord was teaching me to love them anyhow, look beyond their faults and see their needs. Take them where they are at.

Jesus reminded me that He loved me when I was His arch enemy, meaning I was the one that put Him on the cross. Even when they were going by and spitting in his face, Jesus said, "Father, forgive them for they don't know what they are doing." I continued to pray for God's grace, which He supplied, to be gracious to those who weren't being gracious to me. But again, the reason I stayed was because God led me to stay in that community. As it turned out I continued to see fruit born for the kingdom of God: souls were being saved, and the community was being reached for the Lord Jesus Christ. In fact, God even expanded that ministry into not only Hanston and Burdett, but also other towns and rural areas.

After we met for awhile we decided to incorporate into a church. It wasn't just a home Bible Study but indeed God was birthing a church here. We tried our best to leave off a lot of the unnecessary structure that would get so many churches hung up on non-essentials. We began sharing, meeting, and praying and talked about whether we needed a constitution. And then we realized that from past experiences we all had, that people could get to arguing over that constitution and how to interpret it. That would be very limiting and it could put God in a box. So we ended up saying our only written rule for faith and practice is the Bible. Not only did we say that, but by God's grace we sought to be doers of the

27

Word. (James 1:22) Some people wondered what our church doctrine was: it is the Bible. Read the Bible from Genesis to Revelation and you have our church doctrine.

I had never done this before in my life, and it wasn't something I learned in seminary class. God was just leading us along. We are thankful for the wisdom He poured into us in those days. We were determined not to have business meetings where we could sit around and try to out vote one another, debate, and argue. We would get together and we would have prayer meetings and pray until we felt like God had spoken to us. (Acts 1:14) "These all continued with one accord in prayer and supplication, with the women, and Mary, the mother of Jesus, and with his brethren." We would go with whatever God said, rather than go into some business meeting and cast some vote and then ask Him to bless it. I think that is an important principle that churches need to operate on: get before God, seek His face, find out His will, and then do it! You don't have to vote on whether or not you are going to do God's will or not. He will reveal His will—then do His will. It left us a lot freer in our worship service, and we didn't have a bulletin to structure the service.

We did believe that all things were to be done decently and in order; however, we could put the offering first or last or even in the middle, the order didn't really matter. As I said we didn't pass the offering plate anyhow because we were meeting in the house. There was no church building payment. We had to use the utilities in the house anyhow, so there was no overhead to operate the church. One fellow from another city about two hours away came through the community and heard about the house church. He was working for one of the farmers and came by and he was really blessed. He was so impressed with what was going on there that the next Sunday he came back and brought a whole box of hymnals that he donated to us. We handed out some papers with some Scripture songs on them, and we sang those along with the songs from the hymn book. There was such a freedom that we were experiencing there in worship!

We started home Bible Studies through some godly men in the church who sponsored them in their homes. Soon other groups arranged to meet in the various homes. That worked out well, and we got to know each other on a close personal basis in the home groups. We really learned how to pray for one another's needs. It was beautiful how the home groups developed. God was in that too because we didn't have any certain structure in those groups, and God just put them together. We talked about setting aside an evening for visitation to go and visit. We prayed about that, and God said just let each person visit the lost and unchurched on their own time. (Note: This only works if Christians are walking in the Spirit, otherwise laziness can set in and no visitation occurs). If they want you to go along as pastor, they can call you or any others in the church.

We didn't have a membership roll. If you were born again, you are part of the Body of Christ. And if you were coming to this church, you were considered a part of the local body. If you were a Christian and you were attending there, then you were a part of us. (Acts 3:47) "And the Lord added to the church daily such as should be saved." Again, we didn't want to make a bunch of manmade rules even when it came to church membership. (This concept is further explained in Chapter 25—"Random Thoughts".)

We encouraged people to operate in their spiritual gift. We taught some on spiritual gifts. Some people became Sunday School teachers. Some ministered in other ways.

It was a big two story farmhouse, so we used all the rooms. In the worship service we overflowed from the living room into the dining room. Because they were connected in an L shape, I would stand to preach in the middle where the living room and dining room connected so I could see both rooms, although people sitting in those rooms couldn't see each other. People sat on couches and on the dining room chairs. We had to get folding chairs and set them up in the middle. We then overflowed into the kitchen which was open from the dining room. As time passed we overflowed up the staircase from the living room, with people sitting on the stairs during the worship service. By the time we were wall to wall with people, we realized that we needed some more space. We needed a building.

Four and a half years had gone by in the house. I think God saw that we had learned a valuable lesson: church is not a building, and never let a building interfere with anything that He wants to do through the church. A building is merely a tool, a place to get out of the weather, and a place where ministry can go on.

We looked around the community and there was no existing building to rent that we could use. So again we prayed, and God made us of one accord that we were to build a church building. And we wanted to do this as we had the cash. We didn't want to get into debt. We didn't want some bank getting the credit for this building being built. "The borrower is servant to the lender." (Proverbs 22:7) If God wanted the building built, He was perfectly capable of financing that project. Therefore, we would build it in stages, because no man builds the building without counting the cost, so we counted the cost. Luke 14:28 talks about counting the cost before you build a tower. That doesn't mean you have to have all the money upfront. The context is "Are you willing to go the distance no matter what the cost?" (i.e. commitment)

We did it in stages. At each stage, as we had the money, we would do the work. At the completion of that stage, if the money was out, we could quit; it wouldn't deteriorate or rot (good stewardship); we could leave it that way. We could leave it for a while, and not worry about it, and not be pressured for finances, and not have to borrow to finish it. That is what we determined in our hearts that God wanted us to do. Eventually we started looking for land to build the building. We wanted it between the two towns, Hanston and Burdett, and close to the highway.

Some of our people had noticed some ground that looked like it would be a good location. It was a little piece of some farm property that wasn't used for farming because of the way it was shaped. So they thought they would approach the owner who was a Christian man but wasn't in our church. He went to a church down the road. They went to his office and asked him if he would be willing to sell that piece of ground. He asked, "What do you want to use it for?" They said, "We want to build a church on it." He said, "I won't sell it to you, but I will give it to you." So he donated the ground, P.T.L. God was building our faith; He is Jehovah Jireh, the God who provides! He provides in ways we never dreamed. (Jeremiah 33:3) "Call unto me, and I will answer thee, and show thee great and mighty things, which thou knowest not." I could probably write another whole book how God supplied for that church to go up.

We set up a building fund for the first stage, the foundation, and came up with $12,000. Then we began. We were determined to do as much of the labor as we were able to do, only contract out the labor that we weren't skilled in doing. But, being farmers, a lot of the guys had different kinds of skills. The foundation was poured, and we continued building. As I shared, we hadn't passed the offering basket. We had set up an account at the bank and told people, "If you want to give to the building fund, just go to the bank and put it in the Faith Fellowship Building Fund." We had designated a treasurer to keep track of it and to tell us how much money we had to operate with.

If we had the money, we would buy some lumber. A fellow in the next town ran a lumber yard. He wasn't part of our church; he was part of another church, and a Christian man. He called one day and said he wanted to talk to me. He said, "Last night I had a dream, like a vision, and God told me in this dream I was to let you buy building materials at my cost without making any profit on it at all." So we praised the Lord for that, and we got lumber and building materials from him at cost!

We had a retired man in the church, who agreed to be out on the church building site, so that if someone showed up with a hammer and nails, or whatever, he would point them to what needed to be done. Sometimes if we needed something big done, like raising the walls, we would announce it ahead of time, and all the folks would show up at a certain time and get there to raise the walls. One brother had a tractor with a high lift on the front of it to lift up the trusses, and then we would get up on top and nail them down. One brother was an excellent carpenter, and he was on the job a lot. He worked for himself so he was able to come over and donate his time for more technical carpentry needs, and we were right there with him slinging our hammers. I didn't know much about the technical things, but if he told me how long to saw the board or nail a nail, I would do it.

The women got in on it; they painted. I remember when the shingles showed up even the ladies were on the roof, including my wife, putting on shingles. Little kids were below helping carry out trash, or whatever they could be doing. It was a time of working together. I have heard of churches going through a building program end up fuming, fussing, and fighting. But this particular building project just continued to knit our hearts closer together.

We got to a stage in the building where we had given and given. We weren't that big a group. We had doubled in size from forty to eighty people. None were millionaires, and we had reached deep into our pockets as far as we could reach. One Sunday the treasurer said we were out of money and at a standstill. We had already decided that we were only going to build as we had cash, and we weren't going to borrow the money. So, we were in the Sunday morning worship service and praying and saying, "God, we are out of money, and this is your problem. This is your building project and here is the need. We just leave this before you."

While we were yet praying, a woman spoke up. She was visiting her parents who attended our church. She was from Oklahoma where she worked for a doctor, a Christian man, who was aware of our building project. She had an envelope and it contained a check for $10,000! Needless to say, we all rejoiced in the Lord for the instant answer to prayer that we had. God already had the need provided even as we prayed. "The Lord is my Shepherd, I shall lack nothing." (Psalm 23:1 NIV). It goes to show that God finances His programs, and we don't have to look to man, bank, or financial institutions for loans. If God is in something, God will finance it. It may be at the last minute. It was the last minute: we were about to have to call a halt to the progress of the building construction. Now, praise the Lord, when Monday rolled around we were back in there as usual working on the building because we had more money for materials.

After that point we never lacked. We went right on going. A variety of people donated their labor and materials. I remember we talked to a man to lay the carpet in the church because we didn't have any carpet layers in the church. He said he would donate his labor. We needed heating and cooling in the church and none of us could do that. We went to the place that sold heating and cooling units and they said, "We will do the labor for free." Hallelujah! It was interesting as different things were needed in the church, certain people would become a part of our church, as they would move into the community. One fellow moved in from clear across the other side of the state about the time we needed electrical work done in the church. Yes, you guessed it, this man was an electrician! When he came, his father-in-law and mother-in-law moved there also. The father-in-law was a retired electrician. So one thing after another God worked out circumstances on our behalf.

Our God is able. Our God owns the cattle on a thousand hills. If He thinks we need a cow, He will turn one loose out of the herd that somebody else is watching and send it our way. Because our God shall supply all of our needs according to His riches in glory. (Philippians 4:19)

32

And we have a rich God! I know that God honors faith. Faith is not presuming upon God by deciding in your own mind what you want and then expecting God to come through. But faith is discovering the will of God and then trusting Him to do it. In our case it was to build a building, which meant we had to trust God to provide. The same God who leads us into a project will see us through it. "Being confident of this, that he who began a good work in you will carry it on to completion until the day of Jesus Christ." (Philippians 1:6 NIV). God blessed the people in many ways. Some gave a lot, and some gave little, and some gave nothing. God got all the glory, the building was for the glory of God.

It was a rather unique building. The architect of the building, Johnie Guest, donated his services. He lived in Texas. Our family had met his family at a Christian camp. We told him that we were going to build a building. He said, "I would be glad to draw the plans for free of charge," which he did! And on top of that, he took a week of vacation to come and help us during construction!

There was a curved wall on the stage behind the pulpit. We were wondering what we were going to do with this wall. Someone came up with the idea of approaching a famous artist, Stan Herd, out of Dodge City. This artist painted huge murals on the sides of buildings. He agreed for a very nominal fee to paint a mural of a wheat field right before harvest. On one side of the painting it showed the storm clouds moving in and had the verse on the wall, "Behold, lift up your eyes, the fields are white unto harvest." This gave the message of the urgency in getting out the gospel.

I remember how God provided the kitchen cabinets. A train had wrecked and the boxcars were filled with kitchen cabinets. One man in the church bought all the cabinets for a song even before we built the building. When it came time to put them in, he donated them to us. You couldn't even tell they were damaged!

After we got the building built we talked about insuring the building. We thought, "Well, if this is God's building, He is quite capable of taking care of it." So at that particular time in our church's history we didn't feel led to buy any type of insurance on the building. One day a Kansas storm blew in with high winds and hail, it came right over where the church was. The crops were damaged on all sides of the church.

We climbed on top of the roof to check the shingles—there wasn't the slightest evidence of damage whatsoever! So God is able to protect His investments!

We were still operating on no budget, no call for a budget. We still had no overhead. All the money that came in for the building fund went straight for the building. They were still paying me, the pastor, on a love offering basis. If we had any guest speakers or evangelists that came through, we would give them a love offering. We would take up love offerings to send to missions and missionaries.

Since we had been meeting in the house for four and a half years, we had learned not to let the building dictate the program of the church. We didn't change our dress just because we were coming into a church building rather than into someone's home for a meeting. We didn't have to impress people with fancy clothes. There was no dress code. Scripture says that modesty is the rule. Some came in their farm clothes. Some people would wear a tie or a nice dress. It never was an issue because we realized that God looks on the heart, not on the outward appearance. I think God could care less what you wear to church. After all, God cares more of what is in your heart. I have heard it said, on occasion, by some people who think you should dress to the hilt to attend church, "You ought to give God your best and that means you should dress your best, put on your best clothes for Sunday worship." Well that is a partial truth; we should give God our best. I believe giving God our best means He wants our obedience, our service. He wants our heart, and He wants our love, (which I don't see as connected to the style or the quality of the clothing you wear.)

This reminds me of an incident that happened to me in another church. One of our ladies had picked up a hitchhiker, discovered she was homeless, fed her, let her spend the night and brought her to church Sunday morning. The homeless lady put on her best clean clothes. She wore a mini skirt and a low cut blouse. She had a big Harley Davidson motorcycle tattooed on her chest. Her blouse was so low cut you could see half the Harley! One of our deacons cornered me right after church and said we needed an emergency deacons' meeting. There he began to rant and rave about how awful it was that we allowed a woman dressed like that in our church service. He said we should establish a dress code to prevent such people from coming into our doors. I said, "At least she was in church, what better place could she be?" The other deacons agreed with me. I hope when I get to Heaven I see that lady again -- this time dressed in a white robe of Righteousness of the Lord Jesus Christ!

We didn't get hung up on rules and regulations. Rather than having a business meeting, the men would meet from time to time to pray, share our hearts, and share mutual counsel. When issues came up, we would just pray; and whatever we were in one accord about, we would know it to be God's will. I had freedom to be the pastor. So it was rather simple. As a result, a lot of people learned what church is really all about. Getting down to the bottom line, what is church? It is the body of Jesus Christ.

We saw many, many souls saved at Faith Fellowship. It became the largest in attendance of any church in that whole area. To this day, they have continued growing. It is still making an impact for Jesus. It still has the reputation of a church that loves people. A church that will take you right where you are and will accept you where you are; just like God accepts us where we are. God loves me just as I am, but God loves me too much to leave me the way I am. So the Holy Spirit works on us and we have learned to let the Holy Spirit be the Holy Spirit and work. That was Faith Fellowship. Some have gone out from the church as missionaries, and into the ministry, and it still a very strong, vibrant, active, alive church.

But there came a time in my life, when after being the pastor there for about 8 years, the Lord gave me a sense that perhaps He was through with me there and wanted to use me elsewhere. There were certainly no hard feelings or power struggles or anything like that. The church respected their pastor, loved their pastor, and supported their pastor. God was bringing about a matter of change in my life, of wanting to send me to another place to minister.

The call came from a church in Kentucky, Mount Gilboa Baptist Church in Campbellsville. It was a very difficult decision. I struggled with that decision. I was prepared to stay in Kansas for the rest of my life; so was my family. We loved it. The people in the church were not only our brothers and sisters in Christ, they were very dear friends, which is as it should be. Once in a while I run across a pastor who says he doesn't believe that a pastor should get close to members of the church. He should keep some professional air about it.   That's fine for those pastors that believe that, but that is not how God has led me. I believe that some of my closest friends should be within the church.   In fact, I let it be known to any church I pastor that I am available to be among their best friends, fellowshipping in each other's home, going   places together; letting our children play together!   It is just a very neat part of the ministry.

I thank God for my wife and for the role that God has allowed her to play in that aspect. She has the gift of hospitality to have people into our home. She strives to have every family in the church in our home for a meal or refreshments so she can minister to them. It is good for the church to see their pastor as a human being who faces issues of life like they do, and that he doesn't live in some ivory tower.

6.

How to Know the Will of God

At this point let me share a word about how to know the will of God. In my case I was searching for the will of God on whether I should move to Kentucky. How does a person know the will of God?

1. Many times the will of God is already revealed in Scripture. It's right there in black and white. The Bible teaches, thou shalt not kill, thou shalt not commit adultery. The Bible teaches it is the will of God that none should perish, that the way to heaven is through faith in Christ. The will of God is to love one another and to love God with all our heart. The will of God is evident from Scripture in many, many decisions. But the state of Kentucky and my moving to Kentucky are not mentioned in Scripture. Other than Scripture itself, how do we find the will of God?

2. Through prayer, God can speak to us directly by His Holy Spirit. He can directly talk to our conscience, our inner man, He can directly talk to our spirit. His Spirit lives within us. The Bible says we have the mind of Christ, and therefore, many times God can give us a specific word about something we should or should not do concerning His will. God spoke to Paul in Acts 16:9, "And a vision appeared to Paul in the night: there stood a man of Macedonia, beseeching him, and saying, Come over into Macedonia and help us."

About moving to Kentucky, the Lord began speaking to me. At first it was just a sense that I had, a thought that was going through my mind. I hesitate to use the word "feeling," because we are not to be led by our feelings. We are talking about the mind, the renewed mind (Romans 12:2). It went through my mind that God was through with me in Kansas, and He was impressing on me that I should consider going to Kentucky. At this stage it was just a consideration. How else then does God speak to us today?

3. God also uses circumstances in our lives. He uses the things going on around us, supply of funds (I Chronicles 22:5-16), lack of funds (I Kings 17:7-9), situations, open and closed doors to confirm His direction in our lives.

4. Another way God gives direction is through the church and a multitude of counselors. The Bible says in Proverbs 11:14, "In the multitude of counselors there is safety." Going to godly people and asking them what they think about it. I'm not talking about some arbitrary paid professional counselor. I'm talking about somebody whom God has put you in touch with, who allowed your paths to cross, someone who loves you and will tell you the truth and will not try to flatter you. "As iron sharpens iron so one friend sharpens another." (Proverbs 27:17 NIV). Someone whom you believe to be in touch with God, offering godly counsel, not just their own opinion, but based upon firm convictions, somebody whose convictions you trust. One thing you trust is their walk with the Lord - they are walking in the Spirit and not in the flesh. You believe they hear from God. Don't be so proud that you think you never need other Christians. (1 Corinthians 12:21) "And the eye cannot say unto the hand, I have no need of thee; nor again the head to the feet, I have no need of you."

One such counselor I had, God had put into my life since birth. He was also my uncle, L.D. Kennedy. I was saved under his ministry as my pastor. He not only helped me, but his life backed up his teachings. He is the one who gave me counsel to attend Union University and, later on, Southwestern Seminary. He was more than just an occasional counselor—he was also my mentor. By the way, he also wrote a book and inspired me to write this one. If you'd like to learn more of this man of God, and pastor par excellence, read his book: Treasure in Earthen Vessels: Striking Stories from a Rewarding Ministry.

I was talking with a dear friend, Dave Martin, who lived in another state. I mentioned to him I was considering this move to Kentucky from Kansas. I said, "What do you think?" Let me say here when we ask somebody 'what do you think', we are not asking them to be the final voice in our life, but one of many voices, just another source of input that is provided from a godly person. We take that and add it to everything else that God is doing and teaching in our lives. So through Dave's counsel, he quoted Scripture and said, "What you are saying to me reminds me of Acts16:10 where Paul is praying about going into Asia, and got the Macedonian vision in the night, "assuredly gathering that God is calling us to go into Macedonia, we left and went there."" Dave shared that the "assuredly gathering" is like another way of putting two and two

38

together, like when everything lines up.

There were the obvious outward circumstances that Paul had. The guy had appeared to him in a vision and asked him to come over. And the doors had already been shut to go the other way. I might add that open and closed doors is what we're talking about here, circumstances, and that's not to say that every time God closes a door that's not His will. That particular door may certainly be His will, but the timing may be off. In Paul's case he put two and two together and figured he wasn't supposed to go one direction but the other direction by the circumstances.

But an open door doesn't necessarily guarantee that it is God's will. Satan opens a lot of doors. In fact, temptation itself is an open door to sin. That doesn't mean we are supposed to walk through it nor that it is God's will.

So after taking into account Dave's counsel, I thought OK, putting two and two together, what are the circumstances? The outward circumstances certainly led to further impress upon me that God was leading me from Kansas to Kentucky. There's no need to describe those circumstances because it's going to be different in different stages of our lives and different for different people.

I was in Kansas praying one evening. I was walking out in the country where we lived in the wheat field under the beautiful starlit sky and looking up into heaven. I said, "God, I really would like to hear from you; and you know I really don't want to do anything out of your will." May I add here, when it comes to the will of God, if there's a doubt, don't move. You don't have to take one step halfway thinking that something is God's will for your life. You stay where you are in whatever you're doing and whatever situation you're in until you know it is God's will for you to get out of the situation. So don't doubt in the darkness what God had revealed to you in the light. i.e., what's the last word you got from God? Just keep going along and assume you are doing God's will until He tells you that you are not.

Sometimes we make things too big a deal and too spooky wondering if "I'm doing the right thing." Don't worry about it, God loves His children many times more than we love our children. If our children are doing something wrong and is harmful for them, and they are out of our will, we as a parent know perfectly well how to communicate to our children they are out of our will. And God knows how to communicate to us when we are out of His will. Unless God makes it clear to you that you are out of His will, then take it that you are in His will, until such time He tells you differently. (Which in this case He was telling me that I needed to consider changing my pastoral location.)

Now let's get over into the book of James, and we find some further instruction on how to know God's will. Eventually, all may line up like harbor lights lining up when a ship comes into a harbor. If just one light is not in line, the ship is off course, and it may hit a rock or reef or sandbar. Here are 8 harbor lights. James 3:17 says the will of God is "first of all pure." I believe that to mean 'lining up with Scripture'; God would never lead you to do something unscriptural. For instance, someone living in an illicit relationship with someone, an immoral relationship, may say, "Until God tells me it is wrong, I won't get out." Well, He has told us many times it is wrong in Scripture. We don't have to sit around waiting for God to speak to us in a lightning bolt or give us handwriting on the wall.

The next harbor light is "peaceable", meaning God will give us a peace about it. So I was praying out under the stars there in Kansas, and I told God that I didn't have a peace about going or about staying. God reminded me about the godly counsel of my friend and of the Scripture, "assuredly gathering." I started assuredly gathering and putting the two and two together along with all else that God has impressed me with and all the evidence that led that I should go. Although then I did not particularly care to go, and I was not having a particular problem as to why I had to go, because I had a beautiful church and a beautiful relationship with the people. But God finally gave me a peace that I was to leave Kansas to go to Kentucky.

The third harbor light is "gentle" meaning considerate (e.g. how will this affect my wife and kids). No high pressure tactic. Forbearing.

Fourth is "easy to be entreated," or submissive. Christ's yoke (will) is easy.

Fifth is "full of mercy"—compassion for someone in need. Lenient.

Sixth is "full of good fruits"—what kind of fruit will this decision
40

bear? Productive. Unbiased.

Seventh is "without partiality"—no discrimination or favoritism. Unbiased

The eighth harbor light is "without hypocrisy"—is this really me (the new me in Christ)? When I look at myself in the mirror, can I live with this decision? Candid.

To sum it up, God called me to Kentucky and we accepted the call. God was not only concerned about my role as pastor. He was concerned about the rest of my family and how they would be touched by the move. Many times it is so true that the will of God affects so many people. One person may make the decision to respond to the will of God, and many more lives can be blessed. In this particular case, I didn't know why He was calling me to Kentucky other than the fact that He was calling me there.

As it turned out, it blessed my son David, who also questioned why God would ask him to move. He was in high school and had planned on graduating from the school in Kansas where he had been since first grade. He liked his school and he had friends there. He was happy there, and he had no desire to move. However, it was in Kentucky where he met his future bride, sweet young lady named Tricia. It very well may have been if I disobeyed God, I would have somehow short-changed my son's opportunity. But I believe that there are many blessings along the way that we miss out on if we don't cooperate with the will of God.

(You may remember that I said in a previous chapter I asked the Lord about the ability to send my children to college and He told me not to worry about it). When David graduated from high school in Kentucky, he received a very high ACT score, and because of that he was given a full academic scholarship from the college in that town. God had reminded me I had given my children's education over to Him; and God certainly took care of it better than I could have!

Then as my daughter, Gina, graduated from high school in Kentucky, it turns out God moved in her life and provided for her college in a different manner. She won the local Jr. Miss Pageant, and received a full scholarship to go to college! Our God is Jehovah-Jireh, the God who provides! And then our son, Joel, received grants to attend college enough to decide he did not want a college degree.

All along in my ministry I have not looked to man as my provider; therefore, I was not intimidated by churches who suddenly threatened to fire me or cut my salary if I didn't tickle their ears. I believe that every minister of the gospel, in fact, every Christian, should know from day one that God is our source. Our employer is not our source, whether our employer is a church, company, or corporation. We work for God, and we should never be intimidated by Satan through the means of an employer. I believe that we should do a good job for whomever we are working for. Our ministers today would be better off if they would realize this and not allow themselves to be intimidated by man. The Bible says that "I will not fear what man will do to me." (Psalm 56:4). We are to fear God and only God.

Several other things happened while in Kentucky that confirmed to me that we had stepped in the right direction, confirmation that we were in God's will. And even if no confirmation came there, and we didn't see those results and we went there and died there, it didn't matter because what is required for a servant is to obey. What is required is that a man be found faithful. I don't think we can measure success by looking at some outward evidences or see how God is blessing my "ministry" with the world's measure of success. Jeremiah was a very successful prophet of God; by the world's standard he looked like a failure.

So, my Pastor friend, hopefully my testimony and these Scriptures will encourage you in your search for God's will for your life.

7.

Lessons from Kentucky

So God led me to Kentucky to a church way out in the boondocks. You had to be going to this church to get there; it wasn't on the way to anywhere else. As the saying goes, "It was so far out in the sticks, they had to ship in daylight." But God began blessing in that church, souls were being saved; it put a revival in me and the congregation. People began to be excited about the Lord, started inviting their friends. People started to drive out from town to a country church to attend services. God was blessing.

There was no parsonage there, so we were renting a house with the salary we were given by the church. After about a year renting, we got to thinking we wanted a home of our own, because we were happy there and might be there for the rest of our lives. I firmly believe, that, when God leads you into something you should be determined to stick to it until God says your assignment there is finished. Don't leave merely because you receive a more lucrative offer somewhere else. Whatever God is leading us to do; we should be willing to lay down our lives for it. I'm not the type of pastor that uses small churches as a stepping stone, thinking that I will get in a bigger one and then a bigger one and then a more important one. There is no such thing as unimportant churches, as illustrated in the following poem:

"Father, where shall I work today?"
And my love flowed warm and free.
Then He pointed me out a tiny spot
And said, "Tend that for me."
     I answered quickly, "Oh no, not that.
Why, no one would ever see,
No matter how well my work was done.
Not that little place for me!"
And the word He spoke, it was not stern.
He answered me tenderly,
"Ah, little one, search that heart of thine;
Art thou working for them or me?
Nazareth was a little place,
And so was Galilee." --*author unknown*

43

The Body of Christ is the Body of Christ wherever it may be found and whatever size that local body might be. The church is precious to the Lord Jesus. There's no such thing as going up the career ladder in the ministry. Just washing feet may very well be the highest thing you do. The Psalmist said, "I would rather be a doorkeeper in the house of my God." Psalm 84:10. A lot of times, especially in our American society, we put too much emphasis upon man's view of success and importance.

While I was in Kentucky we made many dear friends. We still see each other from time to time. Like the popular song says, "Friends are friends forever when the Lord is Lord of them." The Bible also says, "true love never ends." (I Corinthians 13:8).

It was interesting that in this particular phase of my life, because I had been experiencing at Faith Fellowship a lot of freedom from man's tradition, I realized by going to this church in Kentucky that I was putting myself back in the midst of a lot of man-made traditions. In fact, I reminded the Lord that I wasn't looking forward to that particular aspect. He reminded me that what I felt comfortable with was not my business. It wasn't a matter of my comfort. If only we as Christians can get that through our heads: it's not a matter of what I want and what I'm comfortable with and what I like, it's a matter of being obedient, like Christ hanging on the cross for us. It doesn't mean that to serve God we can't do anything we like, or that it is such a hard task, because Jesus said that "my yoke is easy and my burden is light." (Mt. 11:30).

Some things in the pastorate are humorous. I had only been in Kentucky maybe a couple weeks and preached the Sunday morning sermon. I gave the invitation for people to come forward for any prayer concerns, and this very fragile elderly man made his way down the aisle, hobbling very slowly, shuffling his feet. It took him a long time to get to the front. Finally after he had taken me by the hand, I said, "How can I pray for you, why are you coming forward for the invitation?" He said, "The Lord has convicted me to give up chasing women." I had to bite my tongue! The fellow had to be over ninety and could barely walk. But I went ahead and prayed for him that God would enable him to quit chasing women. And, as I often do when someone comes for prayer, I have the church join in prayer. But I just asked the church to pray, and I didn't get specific. I just asked them to pray for a special need in his life. Later when I was talking to one of the leaders of the church about the man's decision, I said, "Surely he's not chasing women at his age." The man said, "He has quite a reputation for being a woman chaser." Being a pastor can be full of surprises! So be ready to be surprised at unusual times, and ask God for wisdom on how to handle those special situations. Ministry can be a lot of fun!

It was a sweet fellowship there in the church in Kentucky. I don't know any mean- spirited people there. Good, sweet people. However, for the calling that God had put on my life it became apparent that after being there a few years perhaps I had led that church as far as they were willing to be led by me. When I say something like that I'm certainly not knocking that church. They may have been exactly what God wanted them to be. It may very well be that my skills were lacking to communicate and guide the church where it should be. Sometimes God may send another man along that is more gifted in some area than the previous pastor to go ahead and lead the church on through in some area. I'm not the judge, God is. All I know is that for my life there came again a feeling in my heart, unsettledness, unrest. Sometimes the reason you feel an unrest in what you are doing is because God is about to make a change in your life. When He is moving you to something else, He gives you unsettledness in what you are presently doing. That's not the only reason for feeling unsettled. It can also come from Satan, and it takes spiritual discernment and wisdom from God to know the difference. So I began praying about it, "God is this Satan making me feel unsettled here?" Then I started sending out resumes. (It was a common thing for pastors to send out resumes to let the word out they were looking to move.)

I mentioned earlier we had rented a house, but later the circumstances pointed to us buying a house. We were paying rent for about the same amount of money we could be making a house payment and have an investment. Friends I had talked to, including minister friends, said that was what we should do. They said, "When I was through pastoring a certain place, I sold my house and made a profit. It was a good investment." The bank welcomed us with open arms. We had no problem getting a loan on the house we picked out. It all seemed that it was God's will that we buy a house. But every month the house payment got harder and harder to meet. We had to put a few improvements into the house.

For the first time in many years, after being debt free, and experiencing the freedom that being debt free brings, we got ourselves in debt for a mortgage on a home; and that became like a noose around our neck. I am not saying that you should or should not borrow money for a home; that is between you and God. But it appears, as my wife and I look back on it later, that either we missed God when we bought the house, or indeed we were supposed to buy it and learn a hard lesson about finances. I still have unanswered questions about why we thought it was God's will to buy the house. We thought we were doing the right thing. It ended up hurting us financially. When we moved away from there, the bottom had fallen out of the real estate market in the town. Home prices had gone down, and I couldn't get what I had it in. I had to take a loss. So we had to begin the slow climb out of debt. If nothing else, it could have been that God gives grace to the humble and resists the proud. It was certainly a humiliating experience to go through. Maybe He was giving me a more understanding heart for those people who have similar trials.

We started to suffer financially at the church. My salary did not go up to keep up with the needs my family was having. I had to get some part-time jobs to supplement my income—painted houses, sold insurance. I certainly don't put the blame on the church. They were giving me a large portion of their annual budget. Again, I believe that God orchestrates our income, not man, anyhow.

I saw the handwriting on the wall; if I stayed where I was, I was getting deeper into debt with the house. So I began to look elsewhere. For a variety of reasons, God was through with me there at that church. Months went by—nothing. It seemed like Heaven was silent for a while. Sometimes God lets the brook dry up, like with Elijah, to move us on. I began to wonder if God knew where I lived. I began to wonder if there was a church out there that knew I was alive and needed a pastor. You know sometimes when you pray and don't get an immediate answer, you begin to ask, "why not?" Sometimes we don't hear an immediate answer because our lives are out of line and out of God's will, and maybe He won't answer because He does not want to confirm our lifestyle. So He waits until we get in line with Him in some area of our life where we were disobedient, and then He'll answer. Believe me, I did a lot of soul searching and I asked the Lord if there was any unclean thing in me. "Search me, O God, and know my heart; try me, and know my thoughts; and see if there be any wicked way in me, and lead me in the way everlasting." (Psalm 139:23-24). I wanted to be sure I was not quenching the Spirit or hindering Him in any way.

46

There is a variety of reasons we don't get answers to our prayers. Sometimes it is a test of our faith. Sometimes it is a test to help others that God is going to use later on. However, in this case, months went by because it wasn't necessarily things on my end that had to be changed, but that God was preparing another place for me to minister. He was working on the other end in a church in Missouri. The church had gone through some struggles, and things were lining up in that church for me to be their pastor. So the reason for a delayed answer to prayer, in this case, was a matter of timing. God was going to match this move with what He was going to do. He was getting things prepared for that church to receive me and my ministry.

God used my friend, Dave Martin, when I let him know that I was looking for another church to minister in. He gave my name to a church nearby him, New Salem Baptist Church. So, to make a long story short, that church contacted me and said they were interested in me. I had also been talking to two or three other churches. By this stage in my ministry I felt a strong impression by the Lord regarding my next pastorate. I would go into it with my eyes a little more wide open than ever before, figuring I had x number of years to serve God and that God did not call me to a Jeremiah ministry (no converts, no growth, just maintain). God gave me Mark 1:38, where Christ said other towns need the Gospel too.

At this time I was definitely looking for a group of people wanting to be led and who wanted a Shepherd to shepherd them, and who were willing to change if that's what it took. To let the pastor, pastor: i.e. give the pastor leeway to lead. Even though I was hurting financially, I wasn't going to jump at the first thing that came along. Finances should never be the bottom line in changing jobs. Our God is able to supply all of our needs.

There is no need in trying to impose your calling or personality on a church and try to force them to conform to you, for a church has its own calling and ministry. Nor is it necessary for a church to try and force a pastor to conform to them, for he has his own calling. So after this becomes evident, consider that term of pastoring to have accomplished its purpose and move on.

47

God knew that my gifts and calling matched with what that Missouri church needed, and they were willing to follow. After further communication with that church and the pulpit committee, it started to be apparent that that was the direction God wanted me to go. The Pulpit Committee came and found our little country church to hear me preach. My wife and I drove to Missouri to preach in that church and talk with the people. We were looking for God's will and we wanted to be 100% sure that this was indeed God's will. So we looked for what I call "red lights" – which the Spirit of God would flash a red light to say, "No, this is not for you, if this doesn't fit your calling."

I would ask penetrating questions like: Are the deacons willing to "deac", and willing to serve and be willing to minister to families, and be servants to the families under the direction of the pastor? But the deacons weren't doing that at the time. They were just a board who met and made decisions, and then they would bring it to the church for their stamp of approval. They assured me that they would be willing to be Biblical deacons. I said, "That is good to hear. That is what I believe about the role of the deacon." My understanding was that if they called me to be the pastor, they would let me be the pastor. The pastor is the main leader and the shepherd of the flock.

They said they wanted a strong leader, and this is the calling that God has put on my life. To be a pastor that doesn't follow the wishes of the flock but go to God and find out what God wants and then strongly lead the flock in that direction. Again, not knocking in any way how another man feels called or operates.

Sometimes when you are vacillating (it's six of one and half dozen of the other), it's OK to put out a fleece like Gideon did to know God's will. My wife and I said to one another, "Well, we don't have the money to move, and if they are willing to pay for our move, if they really want us there, and God wants us there, we'll trust and put out this fleece (of moving us)." They did get a moving company to pack us up and move us. We said tearful goodbyes to those precious folks in Kentucky, and God closed another chapter in our lives.

8.

Lessons from Missouri

So, New Salem Baptist Church in Winfield Missouri called me and I accepted. I saw that some changes needed to be made there. But the Bible says, "Only a fool answers a matter before he hears it out." (Proverbs 18:13). Some facts can be obvious about a church; for example—history, reports, figures, attendance, budget, etc. Some facts may be under the surface; people's feelings and the spirituality of the church, etc. Proverbs 27:23 says, "A good shepherd knows the state of his flock." So, visit with the people, and get to know them personally, as well as do your homework of reading church statistics.

We started getting the fluff (non-essentials) out of the church service. There is a time and place for everything as Ecclesiastes says. Some things may not fit a particular worship service; birthday songs, announcements, and reports that don't affect the whole congregation. To do this, enlist the help of the worship team, but first get the leadership on board as to what are the priorities in the worship service, so that the fluff can be defined. Worship includes: the preached Word, prayer, music, etc. Churches may differ as to what should be included.

We worked on being intentional; for instance, we needed a visitation-outreach ministry. Don't just say we need to visit, but explain how we go about visiting. This is a part of the pastor's role as an equipper. Not that the pastor organizes all of this, but he gets someone to do it. Make sure all the body is being ministered to: old, young, married, single, new converts, advanced Christians.

If you have to get into a controversial discussion with a member, have a witness present so that that member cannot misquote you. Be a team player. An acrostic for "team" may be: together everyone accomplishes more. If a church has written policies, obey them. If they need to be changed, do so. Work through the chain of command in a church. Run things through proper channels, and committees, and ministry heads. For example, in Acts the deacons were appointed to "be over this business" (serving tables). I taught on spiritual gifts and how that applies to where someone serves in the church.

One Fourth of July on a Sunday afternoon, our son Joel had his friend Josh over to our house to shoot fireworks. The evening service started and they came in and sat near the front. During the invitation a man came forward and was tearfully sharing how God was dealing with him. At that moment we all heard a loud, "Bang, Pop, Bang" – sounded like a machine gun going off in the sanctuary! What had happened was Josh had stuck a package of firecrackers in his pocket, and during the invitation he must have gotten bored standing there. He had his hands in his pockets, like a typical boy and nonchalantly flicking his Bic lighter. The sparks set the whole package of firecrackers on fire. Smoke was pouring from his pocket, and he was jumping up and down, his eyes big as saucers! One man in the back row thought someone was shooting a gun so got down on the floor under the pew. Everyone was looking around and finally noticed Josh backed up against the wall in shock. His mother said to her husband, "Dave, I think you better go over and check on your son." Dave escorted Josh out to the lobby. He was o.k. except for minor burns on his leg, and a ruined pair of jeans!

Back inside the auditorium there was total silence. People were biting their lips to keep from breaking out into laughter. Then the man who been testifying said, "Where was I?" I said, (don't ask me how I could even remember), "You were saying such and such." He then finished his very heart-rending testimony. God impressed me to continue the invitation, and a teenage girl, Christina, came forward to be saved! I asked her what prompted her to come forward after all that commotion. She said, "Well, during the first part of the invitation I heard two voices. One voice said, 'Go forward.' The other voice said, 'Don't go forward!' After the firecrackers, both voices said, 'Go forward!'"

Pastor, it just goes to show you that God is bigger than any interruptions in life. The next day I attended our weekly associational pastors' meeting. As I walked into the room, all the pastors began to sing, "It only takes a spark to get a fire going"! I'm so glad God interjects some laughs during the serious business of pastoring.

We called Mike Steck as our youth pastor with no guarantee that we could meet his salary. We called him by faith, and he came by faith. Faith is not wishful thinking, but acting on God's Word. His salary was met! Mike was like a pied piper for youth. The youth group grew from twelve to eighty each week! We set records for salvations and baptisms.

50

Through the youth we reached lots of their parents. The youth started going to other churches to do youth revivals. They went on mission trips.

Sometimes people in church who had been volunteers in a church ministry (like youth workers) may be threatened that they are not longer needed or important, since the church has called a youth pastor. The pastor must see to it that the staff under him learns to work with such volunteers. Use them and their talents.

But if a volunteer wants to be the boss and not submit to the direction of the staff, he should get out of their way and let them lead. The pastor must be the strongest supporter of his staff, and vice versa. Soldiers on the front-line watch each other's backs.

Have regular meetings with the staff—formal and informal, set calendar dates, goals, pray together, communicate, etc. Let the staff know their job description given them, and then give them a free hand to do it. I say to my staff, "I'm not going to micro-manage you, but I don't want any surprises." See to it that the staff keeps priorities: personal devotional time, family time, etc. Also help the staff set job priorities; for example, if he is a youth pastor, the youth must come first, and then if time allows secretarial work, ministerial work, computers, Sunday School work, etc. It should be understood that ministry staff is available to you when you need him or her. They work for you. They are your assistant pastors in charge of whatever their title is. (It is different for other non-ministry staff – like secretary, janitor, accountant, etc.) Hold each other accountable – "Here's how you can help me." "How can I help you?"

As for volunteer workers in the church, you be their cheerleaders. Show interest in their ministry, but you don't have to take time to be in all their meetings, or else they would be unnecessary. Do not micro-manage them.

After one Sunday morning worship service one of our ladies said, "Pastor, I have to tell you something funny that happened during the service this morning. My little granddaughter was here today. She is from a Catholic church, and she was playing with her necklace with a crucifix on it. She began to swing it round and round and said, 'Hang on Jesus, you're going for a ride!'"

In this church I learned about church politics. Webster's defines politics: "1. act of government; 2. factional scheming for power." How do you get something done in the church? I even hesitate to use this word, politics. It can have a bad connotation. After all, shouldn't God's people be able to see His will and want to do His will? Should not sheep want to follow their shepherd pastor? But God takes us where we're at. The pastor has to take the church where it is at. This is part of "becoming all things to all men." There is more than one way to skin a cat. Get the right people, (those who are like-minded with you regarding God's plan for the church), into right positions of authority in the church (boards, committees). Campaign your view; this may sound crass, but actually you're not promoting yourself but Christ's will for the church. Paul told Timothy to "put them in remembrance, exhort," etc.(II Tim. 2:14) Make sure it is God's will and not your personal preference.

You have one thing no one else in the church has – pulpit – use it! Put your view in a pastor's column, "Write the vision and make it plain" (Habakkuk 2:2), in the church newsletter, on the bulletin board, share your view one-on-one with people, and in small groups. Find external sources that say the same things as what you are promoting: for example, something Billy Graham or some other well know religious leader has said, literature from other churches who incorporate your views, something printed in your own denomination's literature, something from church history. Teach it in a Bible study series, enlist other members to help you promote it, show the benefits of it. Don't run a negative campaign by putting down your opponent. A half of a loaf is better than none, so maybe offer a "thirty day trial."

Speaking of church politics, it reminds me of what Jim Ryan said (he was a Representative for the state of Kansas and had previously served for a while as a youth pastor). He said that church politics was a lot tougher than regular politics!

On the surface it can look like people are following you. They may agree with you initially, but later their true colors come out. After some time passed, some people did not like the new direction the church was going. We had twelve deacons. Six of them organized a coup against me, had their own private meeting, and wrote a twelve page document expressing their dissatisfaction with me as pastor! This paper was full of false accusations. They called a special business meeting and presented

52

this document to the church members. I spoke to each accusation and explained how they were false. Then a member made a motion that since the pastor had thoroughly explained that this document was false, we should consider it rubbish and throw it in the trash can. Motion carried by majority vote.

Another member made a motion that since these six deacons obviously did not support the pastor and presented a document full of falsehoods to the church, these deacons should be reprimanded and put on probation as deacons until such time as they may repent. Motion carried by majority vote. At that point these deacons got up, left the church and never came back. Their family and friends left with them. It was too bad it had to end like that but something had to give. Deacons' meetings had gotten very tense. They were raking me over the coals and questioning my motives. Amos 3:3 says, "How can two walk together unless they agree?"

When the church isn't in unity, not much progress can be made. God had given me some verses before this particular business meeting. Psalms 35:4-8 NIV, "May those who seek my life be disgraced and put to shame; may those who plot my ruin be turned back in dismay. May they be like chaff before the wind, with the angel of the Lord driving them away; may their path be dark and slippery, with the angel of the Lord pursuing them. Since they hid their net for me without cause and without cause dug a pit for me, may ruin over take them by surprise—may the net they hid entangle them, may they fall into the pit, to their ruin." (Psalm 57:6) "They spread a net for my feet—I was bowed down in distress. They dug a pit in my path—but they have fallen into it themselves."

It was painful but good for me; it made me get into the Word, on my knees, and seek godly counsel. Romans 8:28 says, "All things work together for good to them that love God." The whole deal was painful to the church, but good for the church. It was a backdoor revival. By that I mean that sometimes church has revival by adding more members and people coming in the front door of the church to worship and serve. But another type of revival is when the church receives a cleansing and a purging of members who do not want to go on with God nor follow the pastoral leadership that God has given them. So they go out the back door, never to return. The next Sunday church attendance was down of course, offerings were down, and we had to cut back on spending to meet the budget; even my salary was cut.

What wasn't down was our spirit! After about a year church attendance was up more than ever! Offerings increased to the point where the church was able to reimburse my salary deficit. God is able! The church cannot be held hostage by the devil!

Everything was going great in the church. We were blowing and going again. Then tragedy struck! Our youth pastor and his family were on the way home from church one Sunday evening and were in a car wreck. Mike was instantly killed along with his ten year old son, Jeremy. His wife, Brenda and youngest son Alan were severely injured and rushed to the hospital. They survived, but it was after many months of difficult recovery. Needless to say, this put a big hole in our church. It was like we had been torpedoed. We were taking on water fast. Our church went through a grieving time, but we never really recovered. We lost many youth, some because of lack of such a strong youth leader and others because confusion had set into their minds as to why God would let this happen. At that time many people thought, "If God didn't come through in this situation, why would I think He would come through for me? What's the use?" So as a whole the church began to just coast.

Added to this tragic event for our church were other issues: church politics, cantankerous church members; and battle fatigue set in. As pastor, I could not pull them through.

Wow, this is some heavy reading, so let me interject a funny story that happened. I was in the middle of performing a wedding, and all of a sudden the bride fell forward onto my chest. She had fainted! I held her up and the groom helped me lay her on the front pew. A bridesmaid ran and got a cold wet cloth to put on her forehead. The organist continued to play. After a few minutes, she came to. I said, "Jodie, you don't have to stand back up. I can just pronounce you man and wife right now." She said, "Oh no, I want to go through this." So, she stood up and we finished the ceremony. I remembered what a seminary professor told us. "When you get out there in the ministry, always be ready to preach, pray, sing, or die on a moment's notice."

For a while I tried to do a lot of Mike's job and mine, and burned the candle at both ends. I was on my way home from the church office one day, and I cried out to God about how tired I was and how I just couldn't get it all done. He said, "I never asked you to do Mike's job. So quit and

54

do your own job." I said, "But if I don't do it, it won't get done." He said, "Give the church the opportunity to serve." So I let go of thinking that it all depended on me, and a great load was lifted! That old saying came back to my mind, "God is God, and I'm not." The next Sunday I shared that with the church. I said I was going to stick to my calling; and if they didn't step up to the plate, it just wouldn't get done. Some folks did step up to the plate, but overall we lost ground.

We organized a search committee to look for a new youth pastor. We thought we had found God's man for the job, named Jimmy. He also felt that our church was the place God wanted him to serve. However, when it came down to a church wide vote, he did not get the percentage that the Constitution demanded (I think he needed seventy-five percent but fell just shy of that). This was one of those cases where the majority is not always right (like when ten out of the twelve spies voted not to go into the Promised Land). This was also a case showing that a church can get choked on its own red tape. We learned a tough lesson, however, it was too late to get the youth pastor God had in mind for us. We paid a severe price for that as we never did end up with God's man for the job. But we pressed on, and called a new staff member. Some expected him to be another Mike. I think he thought he could fill the position as youth pastor. But after a while it became evident that it was like trying to put a square peg in a round hole. It did not pan out and he left.

The church still could not recover to its healthy, vibrant position it held before Mike's death. I thought that perhaps one of two things was the reason for this. Either the church members were not listening to God nor obeying His leading, or else I just lacked the know-how to lead them. Something had to give.

Be that as it may, God did some wonderful things at New Salem. A mission that we were helping in Mexico needed money to build their church building that had been destroyed by a hurricane. We didn't have a lot of money in our church funds, and we were saving money to add on to our building. We voted to take $10,000 out of this fund and send it to Mexico. God blessed that step of faith, because within a few weeks He had more than replenished the $10,000 back into our fund! We then began to build our Family Life Center as we had the cash.

We were not a traditional Baptist Church – people would come forward during the invitation and receive physical healing, miracles would occur, some people would clap or raise their hands during the music service. On a few rare occasions someone would fall out under the power of the Spirit, etc. These manifestations of the Spirit became a concern to a few in the Baptist Association which we were affiliated with. They called a special meeting to try and oust us from the Association, saying we were not a real Baptist Church. This did not upset us as a church, because we were determined to continue on in the liberty that God had given us. At the meeting, I was interrogated as to my beliefs. Most of the pastors were convinced that even though our church did not fit the typical mold, we were still welcome to stay in the Association, because we still believed in the basic principles of the infallible Scriptures. I appreciated the fellowship that I had with those other pastors and sister churches. But I learned through this experience that a church should not compromise the way God was leading it in order to yield to the peer pressure of other churches. I also learned that a Southern Baptist Church does not have to have a cookie-cutter mentality. God honored our convictions, and the whole Association was blessed, and many became open to the Holy Spirit.

My wife taught a children's Sunday school class. One day she asked the kids how their week was. Little three year old Audri said, "Our cat had kittens." Elaine said, "Oh really?" "Yeh, but the damn dog killed em!" The other kids asked, "What did she say?" My wife immediately changed the subject!

One noteworthy thing that God did in our church concerned a bar in our area. The owner of that tavern got saved. He attended our church and came forward during the invitation to publicly confess faith and request baptism. The rest of his family got saved as well as some of his employees. I baptized them, and they became members of our church. A couple of months later, in a deacons' meeting, two deacons expressed concern that the bar owner still ran the bar but was a member of our church. They said that we should excommunicate him from our church. I told them that I had talked with him about his bar. He informed me that God had been convicting him about selling alcohol and enabling people to get drunk, knowing its devastating effects. But his problem was he had signed a lease on the building. He had contacted the owner, explained to him that he had become a Christian, and wanted out of the lease. But the

56

owner told him if he broke the lease he would have to pay an exorbitant amount of money. The bar owner said that his parents had put up their family farm as collateral for the lease. If he broke the lease, his parents would lose their farm.

When I informed those two deacons of the situation, they said they did not care about his personal situation, and that he should've thought of that before he joined our church. They said that his ownership of the bar was a bad testimony, and that he either get out of the bar or get out of our church. Another deacon spoke up and said that if we really cared about this brother and his family; and if it was really all that important that he get out of the bar, then there was a simple solution: our church could pay off his lease for him. The two deacons said there was no way they wanted our church to do that. The one deacon told them that if they weren't willing to put their money where their mouth is, then they loved their legalism more than they loved their brother. The rest of the deacons agreed with him, and we decided that the best course of action was to pray that the building owner would let him out of his lease. We informed our brother that we were praying for him and the situation, for God to do a miracle, and change the heart of the building owner.

A couple of months passed, and the store adjoining the bar had a water leak that spilled over into the bar and flooded it. The owner of the store was the same man who owned the building that the bar was in. Our brother approached the owner and told him he did not have to pay for the flood damage if he would let him out of the lease. He let him out of the lease! God answered prayer. God then opened up a better business opportunity for our brother.

The point I am sharing this, Pastor friend, is that you may face a similar situation in your church. You may have a member whose testimony is not what it should be. Galatians 6:1 tells us that if we see our brother overtaken in a fault we should seek to restore him in the spirit of meekness. We should spend time with that brother, disciple him, pray with him. We should give the Holy Spirit time to teach him and convict him.

We should do all that we can to help him have a better testimony. Remember how gracious and merciful God has been with you? In a biological family you don't expect a baby to be potty trained until he is

57

about two years old. Why should we expect more from spiritual babies in the church? But after a time, when the baby has had time and teaching to grow, if he persists in wrong behavior, there is probably rebellion involved. Only then should church discipline be used.

The fact of the matter is that those two deacons had a worse testimony than the bar owner. They had been Christians a long time and should have known better than to operate in such a legalistic, judgmental spirit with such lack of love for the brother. They had made no effort to reach out to the brother to help him; they only wanted to judge him. They were more concerned with some pious image that our church might project, when in fact our church projected the image to the community that we loved people "just as I am." More lost people, and people with hang-ups, started attending our church knowing they would be accepted and loved!

After being at this church for fourteen years, I received a phone call from my previous church, Faith Fellowship, in Kansas. They said they needed a pastor and would I consider coming back there to pastor again. I had been sensing that God was about to make a change in my life and wondered if this was it. Elaine and I prayed about it but were getting no specific answer from God.

At this time Kansas was experiencing a severe drought, and the sun was scorching the land. One day as Elaine was doing her routine Bible study, one verse in particular jumped out at her, Isaiah 58:11, "The LORD will guide you always; he will satisfy your needs in a sun-scorched land and will strengthen your frame. You will be like a well-watered garden, like a spring whose waters never fail." She immediately called me on the phone and said, "Honey, I think God has just answered our prayer!" I agreed with her that God had just given us the answer from His Word. However, our children and grandchildren lived near us, and we did not like the idea of moving far away from them to the middle of nowhere. We were not going there blindly; remember we had traveled this road before.

So, like the Psalmist David, I had a little talk with God. I told Him, "God, if you're going to move me so far away from my kids and grandkids, I would like the assurance that you will make it worth my while. I'm not getting any younger, and I don't want to move to the middle of nowhere just to spin my wheels, go through the motions, and see little fruit." God assured me that He would make it worth my while.

So I called the Kansas church and accepted their call. We had mixed emotions. Joy, that God had answered our prayer for direction, but sadness in leaving such wonderful friends that we had made at New Salem. We gave them two weeks notice, in which time there were many tears of goodbye. To this day we still maintain friendships there.

9.

Back to Kansas

Faith Fellowship hired a moving company to pack our belongings and transport them to Kansas. Within two days of arriving in Kansas, God did indeed show me that it was worth my while to move there. A man in the community asked for an appointment to talk with me. He was a Christian but got to the place in his life where he felt disconnected from God. After counseling and praying with him for about an hour, he got the victory! He joined our church and became an avid worker in the Kingdom. Within two more days a couple on the verge of divorce came for counseling, and God restored their marriage! Within a few short months the church doubled in size and has doubled again since! The church was supporting two missionaries, now ten. It's about to be eleven. One of our young couples has felt God's call to become missionaries and they are presently making preparations to go.

We foresee the need for more space (building and parking). We approached the owner of land next to us and asked if he'd sell us a couple of acres. He said he would give it to us! So, God did it again—supplied our every need.

As we continue to grow, it became evident we needed a youth pastor. We did not have enough money in the budget to pay a full-time salary. But we sensed God's leading to step out on faith, even though it did not work out on paper. We found a man, Doug Ellison, interested in the position. We explained to him that we did not, at present, have all the funds to pay his annual salary. We believed that if this was God's will, He would supply. So, by faith, Doug accepted the call. Several years have passed, and he hasn't missed a paycheck yet! Our God is not broke! God not only supplied the extra funds for Doug's salary, but He also supplied thousands more for the youth program!

But wait, I am not done bragging on God. God gave us a bonus. Doug has a talent that I don't have – he is high tech savvy. He helped us install a new sound system and website. As of this writing he is helping us get some big-screen TVs to enhance our worship time. He is securing a camera so our church service can be on TV in order to reach out to the community.

Remember I said we did not have the money to even call a youth pastor, let alone pay for all these projects? This reminds me of a similar story in the Bible in I Kings 17. There was a time of economic recession in the land (just like in America today). The poor widow of Zarapheth said to Elijah in verse 12, "And she said, as the Lord thy God liveth, I have not a cake, but an handful of meal in a barrel, and a little oil in a cruse: and, behold, I am gathering two sticks, that I may go in and dress it for me and my son, that we may eat it, and die." Verses 13-14, "And Elijah said to her, fear not; go and do as thou hast said: but make me thereof a little cake first, and bring it unto me, and after make for thee and for thy son. For thus saith the Lord God of Israel, the barrel of meal shall not waste, neither shall the cruse of oil fail, until the day that the Lord sendeth rain upon the earth." So the widow stepped out on faith and obeyed the voice of God. Verses 15-16, "And she went and did according to the saying of Elijah: and she, and he, and her house, did eat many days. And the barrel of meal wasted not, neither did the cruse of oil fail, according to the word of the Lord, which he spake by Elijah." A church should not focus on its limited resources but on its unlimited God!

I had just come home from our church's annual meeting. (Notice I did not say business meeting). Praise reports were given for what God had done through the various ministries of our church in 2011. Visions were shared by members for what they envisioned God doing in and through our church for 2012. One of our families, who have to drive twenty five miles to church, shared their vision of our church starting a new mission church in their town this year! If you want to keep up with what God continues to do here, you can look at our website: www.faithfellowship4you.org.

Once a year the church would send me on a mission trip, usually to a Spanish-speaking country since I'm fluent in Spanish. The church has funded many special mission projects in those countries. We helped start a mission church in a nearby town. The church even gave me some sabbatical time to write on this book!

The church did not have any elders, so I taught on the subject, and now they have a team of elders to help with the spiritual concerns of the church. Nor did they have any deacons to help with the physical concerns of the church, but now they do. Time does not permit me to share all of the marvelous ways how God made it worth my while to pastor Faith

61

Fellowship a second time. And this time I did not have to shovel hog manure to supplement my income, for they give me a full-time salary. As of this writing, I'm still their pastor. Visitors to the church often comment on how they can feel God's love there, and see the power of God at work.

Faith Fellowship is indeed a New Testament church. Every pastor should have the opportunity at least once in a lifetime to pastor such a church. Oh, it's not perfect. There have been struggles, for instance, music styles.

For the last year of her life, my dear mother was a member of our church. At eighty seven years old she didn't care for some of our new-fangled choruses, or for how some folks didn't wear their Sunday best. But more important than her traditions was her love for the lost, her joy in seeing kids, teens, and young families in the church. She delighted in the mission efforts of our church. I never recall hearing her say, "We've never done it that way before." She believed like Paul, that we must become all things to all men so that some may be saved.

Some other struggles were about the length of the worship service, me preaching in a diaper (to illustrate a baby Christian), budget expenditures, etc. But rising above all such differences of opinion, the church has chosen to love God with all their heart and to love one another. They are determined to not let Satan detour them with peripheral issues but rather to keep Jesus the main focus and advance the Kingdom. There are still areas of growth needed, but they are on the right path, open to God's leadership. Even though the population continues to shrink in this rural community, the church continues to grow and reach lost souls. God may leave me here until I die, or He may have other plans for me. I like the old hymn that says, "Ready to go, ready to stay, ready to do His will." ("Ready", by Charles Tillman, 1903)

10.

If a Church Calls You as Pastor

If a church calls you to be their pastor, you never want to hear these words, "We've never done it that way before." If they aren't willing to make changes, such as God might give them along the way, tell them not to call you as their pastor. Share your heart with that church on your vision, what your ministry is, letting them know up front, no holds barred, nothing hidden, as to what your approach to pastoring would be and what you believe the role of pastor and church are. And let them know that if God was in this and you were called to be their pastor, that you would preach the Word of God as He gave it to you, without watering it down, or tickling anyone's ears.

If you ruffle anyone's feathers, and someone didn't like their feathers being ruffled, or if for some reason they can't be happy with your role as pastor, they need to change their attitude and get over it! If a cat gets upset if you rub its fur the wrong way, it needs to turn around! (That's called "repenting"). This is true unless I am doing one of two things, and that is violating Scripture in preaching heresy or living an immoral lifestyle. But if it's just that you don't like what I am preaching and how I am leading the church because you believe differently, then you need to move your membership to another church. That's a lot easier for you than for me to pack up my family and have to move. I believe if other pastors had a similar boldness their tenure could be a lot longer, as well as that of the future pastor, because the critics would be gone from the church. Don't mistake what I'm saying; I'm not talking about some kind of cockiness. What I mean is, if you know God wants you there, you stick in there until you die or they physically throw you out.

Let me interject a word here about the pastor handling church conflicts. The pastor should keep his eyes on Jesus, keep his mind on the task; "And Jesus said unto him, 'No man, having put his hand to the plough, and looking back, is fit for the kingdom of God.'" (Luke 9:62). He should not allow himself to be dragged down in petty squabbles but should go on about doing the Master's business and not stoop to the level of those who are pulling against him. And don't get down and fight on their level, but maintain a Christian attitude. I am reminded of the children of Israel when they got to the Red Sea in Exodus 14:14, "The Lord shall fight for you, and ye shall hold your peace."

The pastor should not have to defend himself, even as Jesus didn't, nor did the apostles. This doesn't mean you can't answer questions. You should keep the church informed, especially the leaders. But sometimes there comes a point at which any further explanation or discussion is merely debating and wasting time. Jesus kept his eyes on the Heavenly Father and went about His business doing what He was supposed to do. The pastor should not get disturbed, perturbed, frustrated, flustered, confused, perplexed, discouraged or distressed. Just walk in the Spirit and not after the flesh. Be at peace; just let the Lord take care of whatever He needs to take care of. Christ is the Lion of the tribe of Judah: there is no need to defend a lion, just turn him loose!

Stand strong, stand with your convictions, don't complain, don't murmur, don't gripe and don't let a negative attitude well up in you nor let a negative attitude spill over into other people. Be positive, because you have a positive God. Just stand still and see the salvation of the Lord. Watchman Nee, in a small tract I read years ago said, "Are you serving the house of God, or the God of the house?" Pastor, if you get so discouraged or put out with people that you quit serving, maybe your eyes are on people and not God. To quit is to say that Jesus is just a piece of chopped liver to you. Is He not worthy of your service?

Don't worry about your job; don't worry about what they are saying; don't worry about rumors; don't worry about personal attacks on you. One thing: Jesus didn't defend Himself, but when other people attacked the poor, the oppressed; the prostitute that was caught in the act of adultery, Jesus jumped to the forefront and started wielding the Sword of God. And, as a good pastor, we are to do that. We are to stand for the rights of people; their right to worship; their right to be a viable church member, and member of the community of faith, and the kingdom of God; and not to sit back and let them come under attack by a pharisaical attitude that may exist in the church. So Jesus lambasts the Pharisees, yes, but He didn't go about defending Himself. There were times there was a need for righteous indignation and to stand for causes and, if need be, to stand boldly and confidently.

64

Matthew 12:9-14, "And when He was departed from there, he went into their synagogue. And, behold, there was a man who had his hand paralyzed. And they asked Him, saying, 'Is it lawful to heal on the Sabbath days?' that they might accuse Him. And He said unto them, 'What man shall there be among you, that shall have one sheep, and if it fall into a pit on the Sabbath day, will he not lay hold on it, and lift it out? How much then is a man better than a sheep? Wherefore, it is lawful to do good on the Sabbath days.' Then saith He to the man, 'Stretch forth thine hand.' And He stretched it forth; and it was restored well like the other. Then the Pharisees went out, and held a council against him, how they might destroy him." This shows Jesus healing a man on the Sabbath day.

It's interesting to see the Pharisees' response to Jesus healing and helping someone—an actual miracle. Their response was how they might kill him. This can also happen in your ministry as a pastor as you help people, as God uses you to help them find deliverance, salvation, healing, and even seeing miracles take place. Pharisees will respond to you today just as they did in the day of Christ. It's almost like they're saying, "Don't confuse me with the facts." In other words, it doesn't matter what good you're doing or how you're advancing the Kingdom of God. A Pharisee will oppose you just as they did Jesus. So don't let that surprise you.

11.

Being a Shepherd

Speaking of the pastor being the shepherd, if the sheep could lead themselves, then why do they need a shepherd? A pastor's role is to lead the sheep, and not let the sheep lead the pastor. It's not that the pastor doesn't care about the sheep, he does. It's not that he doesn't address their needs, he does. Just like our relationship with God: there is a difference between our needs and our wants. Sometimes we get mixed up, and sometimes the sheep even get confused on what they need. What they think they need may not be what they need. A wise shepherd will know what the sheep needs. He speaks the wisdom of the Great Shepherd of the sheep, and seeks God's will on how and where to lead the flock. It's just a matter of the good of the flock; it's not a matter of the pastor wanting his own way. But he wants what is best for the flock.

The Shepherd Paul wanted what was best for the church at Corinth. But he let them know that his approach, method, and tactics of how he would lead them depended to some degree on them. (I Corinthians 4:21) "What will ye? Shall I come unto you with a rod, or in love, and in the spirit of meekness?" Of course, he would rather deal with them in a gentle manner – just as God desires to deal with us. Psalm 32:8-9, "I will instruct thee and teach thee in the way which thou shalt go; I will guide thee with mine eye. Be ye not like the horse, or like the mule, that have no understanding, whose mouth must be held in with bit and bridle, lest they come near unto thee."

But pastor friend, if you ever do have to use "tough love" with the flock, remember the principle in Ephesians 6:4, "And, ye fathers, provoke not your children to wrath, but bring them up in the nurture and admonition of the Lord." And even though sometimes Paul had to speak sternly to the Corinthians, he took every opportunity he could to please them (not in the sense to curry their favor, but to show them tender love and care). I Corinthians 10:33 says, "Even as I please all men in all things, not seeking mine own profit, but the profit of many, that they may be saved."

The shepherd sees that the sheep are led to green pastures. He knows where the green pastures are. He knows where the green grass is and what

66

kind of grass to feed them. It boils down to the fact he loves his flock supremely, even lays down his life for the sheep. Now that doesn't mean he gives in to their wishes. Laying down his life means that he lays his life on the line doing what he believes is best, just like Jesus did for us. And He laid his life down even though His disciples didn't understand what He was doing, and said He shouldn't die. (Matthew 16:21-22). They thought He was pursuing a wrong course of action. Yet He went ahead and laid down His life for His sheep.

Even well meaning church members sometimes try to tell the pastor how to pastor, and say, "Because I love you and care for you; you are going to ruin your ministry here.", etc. Do they really mean that or are they just saying that for their own agenda? Or they may really care just as Peter did for Jesus, but Peter wasn't quite as informed as he should have been. I believe if anyone is informed it is the pastor. God is going to give him, of all people in the church, wisdom and direction on the way the church should go. It's not that other people can't have some words from God, but they should all come under the leadership of the pastor.

Luke 6:26 says, "Woe unto you, when all men shall speak well of you! For so did their fathers to the false prophets." The pastor should not expect everyone in the church to always appreciate his sermons or the way he is leading the church, nor should any Sunday school teacher or anyone else in spiritual leadership in the church. Even parents catch flack from other parents sometimes when these parents are leading their children in a way they don't care for or understand. The main thing is that we hear the words, "well done thou good and faithful servant." (Matthew 25:23).

It's one thing to have a listening ear and to carefully and prayerfully weigh what people share with us. But the bottom line is there are going to be some people that will not speak well of us, and there is nothing we can say or do to please them. Even if we could please them, they will think of some new thing for which to criticize us. It's not our task to try to make people speak well of us and get the approval of men. Nor is it that we are trying to go out of our way to get people to disapprove of us. I have observed some pastors that go out of their way to make people mad at them, just to be different for the sake of being different. They have a martyr complex, and say, "People don't like me," when quite frankly, the personality of the pastor had gotten in the way. A pastor's pride or stubbornness is something a pastor has to guard against.

Members should love, respect, support, pray for, and obey the pastor when he is following Christ. But pastors are not perfect, so sometimes members should disagree with us, but lovingly and respectfully.

In Galatians 2:11-14 Paul publicly rebuked Peter before all the church at Antioch, because Peter was showing respect of persons.

In Acts 18 Aquilla and Priscilla corrected and instructed Apollos on his inadequate view of baptism.

Ezekiel 34 is a strong indictment against the shepherds of Israel who were not doing their job but were neglecting and sinning against their flocks.

I read an illustration about a shepherd taking care of some sheep in a country where they still have lots of sheep. The shepherd had a particular rebellious sheep that kept straying off from the herd, wouldn't stay in the green pasture and still waters where the shepherd had him. He kept crossing the fence to the other side. The shepherd would go get him and bring him back. There is that principle where Jesus would leave the ninety-nine and go for that one lost sheep and bring him back rejoicing. However, when the shepherd brought this one back he knew that in a few days this sheep would be right back out of the territory again. So this shepherd broke the sheep's leg. Pastor, to be honest sometimes you feel like breaking the legs of a rebellious church member! Basically, it means not letting him have his way. He will scream and holler when this happens. But the shepherd, after he breaks its leg, would then carry it around. He will develop a close relationship with the sheep and give it special tender loving care. After that, once the sheep was healed, it would never stray again. Finally it knew it could trust its shepherd!

12.

Who Does the Church Belong To?

Who does the church belong to? The church belongs to the Lord Jesus Christ, who is to be the head of the church, (Ephesians 4:15), who is the boss of the church, who runs the church. In contrast, there are in many of our churches good people who sit back and do nothing about allowing men to run the church. One way a nation falls is that good men do nothing. It's not that good people in the church become wicked and start sinning and doing bad things. Good people in the church may, for whatever reason, sit back and do absolutely nothing while allowing a handful, (one, two, or three selfish people) to give direction to the church and basically control it. They even try to control the pastor and in any way God is leading the church through the pastor. Good people should not allow this to go on! Good people should rise up and say, "We aren't going to take it (the backbiting, the gossip, negative talk about our pastor and what God wants to do and the changes God wants to do in our church) anymore. We are not going to submit to man's leadership; we are going to submit to the leadership of the Lord Jesus Christ." They should rise up and stand behind the pastor on how he is leading the church.

Most churches can rise above this age-old problem of man wanting to control the church. There is a time for good people to arise and stand together behind the pastor and speak up. Don't allow a few mouths that are very verbal to intimidate good people! You may think, "Who am I to say anything? These people have been in our church a long time, may even be founding members of the church. How can I speak out against them?" I'll tell you how to speak out against them. They are speaking out against God's leadership of the church. It's time to tell brother and sister so and so, "No matter how long you've been here, how much money you give, what offices you hold, we are looking to God to direct this church, to lead this church, to guide this church. We aren't looking to you or your handful of cronies."

III John 9-10, "I wrote unto the church, but Diotrephes, who loveth to have the pre-eminence among them, receiveth us not. Wherefore, if I come, I will remember his deeds which he doeth, prating against us with malicious words; and not content with that, neither doth he himself receive the brethren, and forbiddeth them that would, and casteth them out of the church." So intimidation is used, lies are being used, lies being told on the pastor, rumors and gossip planting suspicions in people's minds. The devil uses fear tactics, fear of what may happen, what we may come to, (e.g., we may lose our entire heritage). Some people even plant land mines in their own church, so that someone else will get the blame. They will quit attending and say, "look how the attendance has dropped." They will quit giving and say, "look how our giving has dropped." They make it reflect badly on the pastor.

They will even destroy their own church. They will cut off their nose to spite their face. Many are like a dog in a manger: if they can't get in on the blessing, they don't want anyone else to. A mean dog will stand in a manger (trough) of hay and bark, growl, and snap at a cow approaching the manger to eat the hay. The dog doesn't even like hay, but it doesn't want the cow to get any.

Another reason people act ugly is they may be convicted and don't want to repent or change their ways. They don't like the message so they discredit the messenger. It's amazing that disgruntled church members who aren't happy want others to be unhappy with them. Birds of a feather flock together—-they want others to go down in misery with them. Proverbs 16:29 says, "A violent man enticeth his neighbor, and leadeth him into the way that is not good." They try to make others miserable in casting these suspicions, doubts, and accusations against the pastor and what God is trying to do. Even sometimes they call the works of God the works of Satan, (Luke 11:14-20), bordering on blasphemy itself, just because they don't understand it or they have never experienced it or they can't explain it. It goes against their pet narrow system of theology and doctrine that they have.

Good people should not allow a few bad people to run the church, run it into the ground, run amuck, and in fact kill it. I have heard people say sometimes, "Oh pastor, we love you; we don't know why you've left." After I resigned from the Hanston church, one lady said, "Pastor, I was for you." I said, "Well, it's too late to speak up; you should have spoken up earlier. I wouldn't have left, and you could have gotten rid of the cancer that was in your church. It's a cancer when men try to control the church and run it man's way. It's a little late now." When good people to do nothing is as sinful as the evil people who rise up and do something.

70

Just like in our land, there are enough good people and Christians in America to win our nation for Christ and to turn our government around, but many do nothing. They don't vote, they don't check out the candidates, they just sit back and do nothing. When they don't do anything, weeds grow. It's time for weed pulling in our churches – not that we can ourselves separate the tares from the wheat. That will be done in the end time. There will always be a mixture, but as much as you know how, when you are sure it's a weed in your garden, pull it out. Pull such people out of positions of leadership in a church. They may be welcome to be members but they don't need to set the agenda, and they don't need to be given leadership positions. Their voices don't have to be heard and heeded – a little weed pulling, a little thinning out to remove the weeds of misguided ignorant leadership that has no vision and doesn't want to go on with God. If they can't lead, they shouldn't be in a position of leadership.

Sometimes you will have people who are hidden leaders (a Jezebel spirit), who don't have any big titles but they stir up trouble behind the scenes. I have seen many a man ruined because his wife wasn't in submission to him, and she was running the show behind closed doors. He may have had a position in the church, but he would have to check with his wife every time he needed to make a decision in the church. So there is some behind the scenes weeding that needs to be done and exposed. But let me warn you: when you start exposing Satan, and start exposing his lies, you will make the devil mad! He then knows his days are numbered, and he fights tooth and toenail with his claws. He pulls every weapon out of his arsenal that he knows how to throw.

I Peter 4:12 says, "Think it not strange my brothers concerning the fiery trial that you are going through." When you are trying to follow Jesus, Satan will come against you with his weapons. Don't let that shock you, don't let that surprise you. Don't think that something is wrong. Don't let it make you think that you aren't going the right direction. It means you are going in the right direction, because you are butting heads with Satan himself. And he doesn't give up easily. He tries every trick he knows how to apply. His biggest trick is to get inside the church, not attack it from the outside by setting off some bomb, but trying to get into the hearts and minds of members and have them carry poison (a poison of a bad report, against one another, backbiting). Galatians 5:15 says, "Be careful how you are backbiting and consuming one another with all your backbiting."

Therefore, we must be aware and alert, because our adversary walks around like a lion that's seeking whom he can devour. (I Peter 5:8). He comes to steal, kill and destroy (John 10:10); we need to recognize him. We need to call his hand, don't be afraid of him. Hit him head-on. Many people don't want a conflict. Some people settle for deadness quicker than they will deal with conflict and controversy and a fight, because they would rather run. Many a good person has run out of a church because he doesn't want to stand.

Ephesians 6:12-13 says, "For we wrestle not against flesh and blood, but against principalities, against powers, against the rulers of the darkness of the world, against spiritual wickedness in high places. Wherefore, take unto you the whole armor of God that ye may be able to withstand in the evil day, and having done all, to stand." That's what we need to do in our churches – for our members to put on the full armor of God and stand against Satan, because we are already guaranteed that we are going to win! We don't have to be afraid. It may be tough, and the arrows will fly, but if we hold up the shield of faith, the arrows won't penetrate us. Don't be surprised because you hear the bullets zinging by. We are in war, and bullets will fly!

Many people, because of their lack of commitment to Christ, just want a comfortable Christianity, and so they try to keep peace and kept things "smooth" in the church. They won't stand against evil when it comes in. They just gloss it over and say, "Well, we all have to get along," and they know they don't need to ruffle so and so's feathers, because he gets madder than a wet hen when you do that. You'd think that that somebody who's going to get madder than a wet hen because you ruffle his feathers doesn't need to be in a position of leadership! But instead of saying anything, the church often keeps pampering some big spiritual babies who whine if they don't get their way. They need to call their hand! But they want to run and they want to put their head in the sand. I'm talking about good people who want to put their head in the sand. They get tired. Galatians 6:9 says, "And let us not be weary in well doing; for in due season we shall reap, if we faint not."

72

A lot of churches get on the verge of breaking through to become the church God desires. One pastor will leave because a handful of selfish, misguided, ignorant, unspiritual people ran off the last pastor, so they get a new pastor and hope he will lead them on; and sure enough he does, at first. The church may start seeing some progress again. New people start coming in. They are about to break through again but it's only a pattern that is repeated over and over. And when those who are the controllers in the church see that they are about to lose that control, then they start the war again. It doesn't matter what the issue is. They start a war on the pastoral authority that has come in, and war against God's leadership in the church. It starts all over again and they put the pressure on until that pastor is gone. That is why the average stay is only two years in many churches.

Unfortunately a lot of pastors get weary and turn tail and run. I would rather go down swinging against Satan and his forces than to turn tail and run. You are likely to run into another church where they haven't broken through either and haven't broken the pattern. And you are going to be there until the honeymoon is over, and it is going to happen to you again. So you might as well get this set in your heart: God called you there and don't you leave until God calls you away! And you keep standing.

But, oh, how weak we have become. We have become weary in well doing and we have gotten battle fatigue. But there are ways to overcome that. We all need to rest every now and then. We all have periods where we need to get alone with God, and go up on the mountain with God. A seminary professor once told our class, "When you graduate and pastor a church, you're going to work hard to do a good job. Just remember to get some rest so you don't burn out. Jesus said to His disciples, 'Come apart and rest awhile.' Class, you can come apart and rest awhile or you can just come apart!" Jesus needed to get away from the crowd; He wasn't running. He was recharging His battery. And that is what we need to do. So pastors, and all Christians for that matter, need to go on a vacation every now and then. They need to go off to a retreat, to conferences, get away from the telephone, get in the prayer closet with God, get godly counsel from others; so do church members. The purpose is so you can continue to stand against the wiles of the devil.

Another reason people can't stand is that they are so out of shape they are spiritually fat. They come to church, sit there and soak in more and more teaching and get spiritually fat. They don't put into practice what they are learning. They have never won a lost soul to Christ. They don't visit prospects. They just come in and sit, soak, and sour. They're just putting spiritual fat on themselves. And the battle gets thicker, and they can't stand up. They run out of breath, and they faint because they don't have much muscle, just fat. Hebrews 5:14 says, "By reason of use have their senses exercised." They can't fight the good fight. Sometimes it's like a big test; you can tell you flunk the test if you faint. Then you are letting yourself know, or God is letting you see, that you only thought you were strong. "If footmen tire you, what are you going to do when horsemen come against you?" (Jeremiah 12:5). It's good to take some spiritual inventory now and then. This inventory should be done not only for you personally, but the local church needs inventoried also; like getting a thorough check-up from Dr. Jesus.

Scripture talks about the reason divisions, strife and problems come upon the church – so they whom God approves as leaders may be made known. "For first of all, when ye come together in the church, I hear that there are divisions among you; and I partly believe it. For there must be also heresies among you that they who are approved may be made manifest among you." (I Corinthians 11:18,19). Sometimes that is a way of testing for someone or a church. We say we love each other. In the church, just have some controversy, and then we will see how much we love each other. Can we love each other in spite of the controversy?

Sometimes it's like a bomb the devil drops in our midst—just like the bomb that exploded in Oklahoma City at the federal building. Satan wants to sneak into our churches and drop a bomb. You can tell who had their armor on and who didn't. Those who didn't have their armor on are full of shrapnel. And they are bleeding, bleating, moaning and whining. Are they hurt? Yes, they are really hurt, but they didn't have to be hurt. That is the point. They should have been wearing the shield of faith, the breastplate of righteousness, the helmet of salvation—wearing the full armor of God (Ephesians 6:14).

Sometimes a bomb is brought into the church by an act of the flesh from some individual (whether it be a member, the pastor, a deacon, an elder, or an evangelist that comes in.) None of those people are perfect. Whenever there is any imperfection that shows up, flesh shows up. What happens when flesh is exposed is that, if you are walking after the flesh, your flesh reacts to that flesh and there are sparks that fly. It doesn't have to be. Someone can act in the flesh, and if you are walking in the Spirit, just pray for him. Realize he isn't going to win. Just go on down the road you are on. But sometimes that doesn't happen. Instead the sparks fly, and just like in the Oklahoma bombing, you need to send in the rescue team to do damage control.

But the ship can still sail on even though she takes a torpedo in the hull. Those who are strong go down and patch the hole, pump out the water, and the ship keeps sailing. The church of the Lord Jesus Christ, the ship of Zion, is sailing on. It's not time for us to bail out and jump ship. It is time for us to patch the hole and do damage control, minister to whomever will receive the ministry, go on through life and sail on for Jesus. You do that and you will be able to take on even more passengers to get in the ship. You love the people and do whatever you can. Some may drown. Some may not let you rescue them. That is their problem. Then that is between them and God.

All you can do is hold out your hand like Jeremiah the weeping prophet. He preached the Word. He shared the Word. Jesus Himself said, "I would have gathered you as a mother hen gathered her chicks under her wing, but you would not" (Luke 13:34), and Jesus wept. And our attitude should be one of weeping over those who are in trouble. Your heart goes out to them just like in any war; yes there are casualties. There are those who get wounded, and there are some who even die. And, yes, you grieve for your fellow soldier who unfortunately takes the bullet. But what you do is respectfully bury them and go on. And you keep advancing the lines against the enemy is. You realize who the enemy is, and that is Satan. And he is the one who shot the bullet at your brother to start with. And it should make you mad at the Nazis or the communists or whomever you are fighting out there in the war. Go ahead and say when you shoot your bullet that "this is for my dear brother who lies slain out there on the battlefield." And we should have such a righteous indignation about us to be able to aim our bullet in the right direction against the forces of evil: go win another soul! That's when it is time to turn around, counterattack and bomb the devil! He is the one behind it. Go make a visit, go do a good deed for a neighbor, go encourage someone, pray for your enemies. Get on the counterattack, get on the offensive, and don't just sit there.

75

Yes, you will grieve for the one left on the battlefield but the war continues. The cause for which you are fighting is still there. We are fighting for the Lord Jesus Christ. We want to advance His church, His kingdom. Jesus went ahead with His mission even though His heart was grieving for those who rejected Him! He went on to the cross and laid down His life for us, and He accomplished the mission for which He was sent. The church is on a mission, and we can't let some misguided, misdirected, selfish individuals get us off track! We must answer to God. We must press on; press in, go forward just like Paul did in Philippians 3:14. We are serving a loving Heavenly Father, and it is Him that we are serving; it is Him that we are trying to please. It is Him we are allowing to live in us and operate through us. We must go on, and we must stand in the full armor of God.

But the good people want a leader, and they want a strong leader. So, God, please anoint many more strong leaders, young men coming up through Bible colleges and seminaries, and middle-aged men who will stop chasing the American dream and start chasing service to God, and old men who may be off the board but not off the Lord, who may have retired but get re-fired for the Kingdom work! May He raise up a mighty army. He is doing it. We are seeing some major changes in the church these days! Thank the Lord for some good, godly, Spirit-filled, strong leaders. That is what the good people want.

So I challenge the good people of the churches: don't be mislead, misguided, hoodwinked by a few Diotropheses in your churches—those that would love to have the preeminence (III John 9). You let Jesus run your church. Yes, there will be casualties along the way; and yes, obedience to God is very costly. The fact that Jesus was born, was that God's will? Yes, that was His will—but it cost a lot, a lot of little boy babies that Herod had slain when Jesus was born because Herod was jealous. It was costly when Jesus was born. Many other times in secular and biblical history when someone decided to follow God all the way, it cost some people around them.

We have to watch that we don't get our sentiment confused and let our emotions get in the way of what God is wanting to do, thinking it is going to hurt so and so, and cost so and so something. That is right, my friend, it cost Jesus His life. His obedience to His Heavenly Father cost Him everything He had. He said it was worth the price for the result: the salvation of our souls, the redemption paid for mankind. Sometimes that is true as the church advances it may cost some people their favorite classroom to move to a different place, may cost the color of a wall, changing the time of the services, certain seat in the choir, music that is not their style. It may cost us something to go ahead and make the adjustment He wants us to make in life. It is worth it, and we must realize it up front. Otherwise it's like children that just want candy for supper. We tell them no. In order to have a healthy body they have to eat their vegetables, meat and potatoes at the supper meal. The little guy will cry and have his feelings so hurt, but we have to understand the difference between some people's feelings being hurt and grieving the spirit of God. There is a big difference.

Don't grieve the Spirit of God, don't act in an un-Christlike attitude or way but go ahead and follow Jesus, no matter the cost. Just like the early disciples did in the book of Acts—they followed Jesus. It cost Paul his freedom. He was thrown in jail. He was following Jesus. I have seen that sometimes obedience to Christ cost somebody their job, and it cost some friendships. Not that you are trying to turn against your friends as you follow Christ. They may not catch the vision with you, and they are going in the opposite direction from you. Mark it down; it will be worth it all when we see Jesus and He looks at us and says, "Well done thou good and faithful servant!" (Matthew 25:21). God didn't call us to be successful; He called us to be faithful. I'd rather die obeying Jesus than gain all the successes of this world but not be obeying Jesus. Be faithful, be faithful, and be faithful, no matter what the cost!

Give the church back to its rightful owner—Jesus Christ!

13.

Faithful Men – A Key to Success

Think of the word "success" and how to have a successful church. You may see one church that grows and has a great ministry. God may lead that church to start a bus ministry, and they really start growing into a great church. And other people come around and ask them, "What was the secret of the success of your growth?" Maybe this church even writes a book on how to grow a great church. The answer isn't the method, but their obedience. Another church may buy buses but doesn't grow the church. Perhaps God isn't leading you in that direction.

You don't have to copy the methods of another church. He leads, obey Him. He has to be the boss, the leader, and the head. Ask Him how <u>He</u> wants your church to operate; how does He want you to operate in your Christian life according to your gifts and callings. Don't follow after other traditions; all that is, is spiritual adultery. We are to have a love relationship with Jesus.

If we had more prayer meetings than business meetings and committee meetings, I believe we would see the power of God fall on us! We would be of one mind and one spirit in seeking the Lord's face, the Lord's will for us as individuals and as a church, and we could operate accordingly, instead of trying to make our plans up and then asking God to bless them. We are talking about having a relationship with God as an individual and as a church. We need to <u>relate</u> to one another. It's almost a forgotten art on how to relate to one another, with the advent of TV, sporting events, computers, and cell phones. We want to be entertained and we don't know how to initiate relating to one another. As we relate to one another, we learn to love one another, walk together in harmony and know that we can pray with one another about things.

Trust one another in the work of Christ. Trust the Lord, because it's that walk with God that gets the job done. He may use us as His instrument. We need to find out where He is working and what He is doing and join Him there. For instance, instead of you trying to figure out what you should preach next Sunday, ask God, "God, what are you preaching on Sunday?" Be prepared and stay free of any encumbrances that would use mental energy that will be needed to be devoted to the

Kingdom. We have to wait upon the Lord as Scripture says and seek His face.

II Timothy 2:2 says, "And the things that thou hast heard from me among many witnesses, the same commit thou to faithful men, who shall be able to teach others also." Seek out other godly men, Paul said to Timothy. Some use the word "mentoring" for this. The concept is like Jesus and the Twelve where He prayed, and after He prayed He selected twelve. Mark 3:14 says, "And He appointed twelve, that they should be with Him, and that He might send them forth to preach." Jesus chose these men not only to preach, but that they could spend <u>time</u> with Him— hang out with Him. It's more "caught" than "taught." He walked and talked with them.

The pastor of the church should do the same. He should pray about who are his faithful men and surround himself with those faithful men. He should seek to spend time with them on a regular basis where he can get to know them more and they get to know him more as a person and a human. He can impart his heart; share his mind, his vision, his goals, his thoughts, and interpretations with these men (which go far beyond what would happen in a Sunday morning service). They could share strengths and weaknesses with one another, pray for one another, support one another. It is too easy for the pastor to go about putting out little fires here and there and be so busy and spread so thin that he isn't taking the quality time he needs with his faithful men.

Why should the squeaky wheel get all the oil? The idea is that the pastor shares with the faithful men; they in turn share with other folks. Therefore, the pastor's ministry is multiplied, rather than the pastor running around trying to do it all. It makes for a more effective ministry. It helps remove suspicions and mistrust. Also it provides for accountability, for sharing prayer concerns, for revealing strengths and weaknesses. It provides moral support and encourages church support.

Once they understand your vision, ministry, and heart they would be more apt to support you. Also the Bible says that in the multitude of counselors there is safety (Proverbs 24:6). And you would be able to bounce ideas off of one another. Rather than only the pastor having an idea or suggestion, maybe one of the godly men does, or has a direction the church needs to go. If you put it out to the whole church to vote on, all that you are doing in that case is putting it out to the crowd. Amongst the crowd there is a variety of immature folks who are casting a vote on which they may have no understanding nor spiritual wisdom. A "majority"—ten of twelve spies—voted not to go into Canaan. Result? 40 years in the wilderness! A majority crowd said of Jesus, "Crucify Him" (Mark 15:13). So, the crowd can promote ideas which have not been prayerfully considered and scripturally checked out. Getting godly men seeking God's face helps to avoid an immature majority or popular opinion running the church.

Also these ideas can be fine tuned, and tossed back and forth, cleared up, etc. in order to be more easily understood by the people. The pastor needs "Hurs". While Joshua was on the battlefield fighting, Aaron and Hur held up Moses' arms, which held up the rod of God (Exodus 17:12). The pastor needs godly men around him to hold up his arms, to be his strongest supporters. So there's a principle in Scripture to have that group of faithful men to do this. The pastor needs to pray just as Jesus did before He picked the twelve. You can't judge a book by its cover, and who you think are your faithful men may not really be your faithful men. They may look like it on the outside. They may look godly.

Another reason there are tests and trials that come to a congregation and among personal relationships amongst Christians is for testing to see who really is a faithful man. (I Corinthians 11:18-19). So much prayer needs to go into the selection of these men, and the pastor needs to explain to the men the purpose. I believe this is the underlying principle behind the selection of church officers, deacons, elders or whatever you call your leadership. If they can't qualify to be a faithful man, they never should have a leadership position. Not that there aren't other good men in the church, but the pastor has only so much time that he can impart, and the group doesn't need to be too large.

And what is a faithful man? A faithful man is a man who has his priorities straight. The first priority is his personal relationship with Jesus (Mark 12:29-31). He is totally in love with Jesus, totally committed to Jesus. His personal walk with Jesus is the number one priority in his life-meaning he gets in the Word, meditates in the Word, gets in prayer, believes in prayer, is filled with Spirit, not filled with self. His goal in his life is for God to get glory out of his life, whatever walk of life he may be in.

The second priority, if he is married, is his wife. He knows how to meet the needs of his wife. He is the spiritual leader to his wife, and he meets her physical, spiritual, and emotional needs.

My wife and I try to have a brief devotional time together each morning in the Word and in prayer. Even as Christ loves the church he is willing to lay down his life for his wife. He nourishes and cherishes her (Ephesians 5:28-29).

The next priority is his children, if he has children. Seek to be a good daddy to his children, to raise them in the admonition of the Lord (Ephesians 6:4). It doesn't mean your kids have to be perfect. God is the perfect Father, but his kids (like me) sometimes misbehave. Love them even as the Heavenly Father loves us, and set a good example in front of his kids—not just preaching to his kids, but living Christ like in front of them. Other ways he can show his love is by spending time with his children, praying with them about their wants and needs, having interesting devotions with them that are age-appropriate, and communicating to his children about all the issues of life.

Lastly then comes career. Whatever that career is—either secular or religious, whether it is a pastor, banker, ditch digger or whatever, seeking to give an honest day's work for an honest day's pay. Not making a god out of a career, but spending a proper amount of time and energy in a career. A career should not get in the way of developing other relationships and ministries that he may have.

Here are some marks of a faithful man: (and remember, pastor, this applies to you as a faithful man also) a man who is rightly related to God (vertically), rightly related to his fellow man (horizontally), having fellowship, discipling, being a friend, encouraging others, admonishing others. A faithful man is a balanced man, with a balanced life. He doesn't get off on tangents, keeping Christ central in all things. He is a man who rightly divides the Word of truth. A man who wants to learn, who doesn't feel like he has arrived, yet always eager and actively seeking to grow by placing himself in the way of blessing and of growth, whether that is formal or informal. A faithful man wants to grow spiritually and seeks to improve himself by God's grace (presses on like Paul). He is also a man

81

who is progressing along the way. God doesn't look at how high up you are on the ladder to maturity, but He looks at what direction you're going!

Some men know a whole lot more than other men about Scripture, and some have studied a lot more. But more importantly is that he is found faithful with whatever God has given him. "Moreover, it is required in stewards, that a man be found faithful" (I Corinthians 4:2). The faithful man doesn't have to be a highly gifted man as the world and religion looks at it. But is his focus on Christ? You can pretty much tell if the man is a faithful man by where his focus is. What does it take to discourage him? Does it not take much to get him down? Does it not take much to get him sidetracked? Then he is not a faithful man.

It is difficult to tell who the faithful men in the church are and who aren't by merely superficial observation. We are not talking about being religious; we are not talking about obeying a lot of laws, rules and regulations. We are not talking about being able to just talk the talk; we are talking about walking the walk. A real key to having a New Testament church is that faithful men lead under the leadership of the pastor, and all under the leading of Christ.

On the subject of faithful men, it is important to look at the various positions of leadership that may come open in the church. People who are in the position of spiritual leadership in a church should be faithful. For instance, if we are looking at who is supposed to be an elder or deacon, or who should be leading a very important program of the church like Sunday School director, leaders of home Bible studies, the policy makers in the church, the trend setters, then those that are in positions of authority and leadership should be faithful. Now, working under them, may be a variety of people, but the faithful can help keep things focused and on track. Of course some positions in the church don't require a lot of spirituality, and you can have whomever to straighten up the pews, set the thermostat, work in kitchen, usher, and things like that.

There are a variety of jobs and tasks that can be done in the Kingdom of God. But those who are in key positions in the church should be filled by the faithful. The pastor should find out who those faithful are and encourage them to get in those positions. Sometimes there has to be some weeding out of people who have been in it for the wrong reasons, the wrong motives, are totally incapable, or who are not spiritually mature enough to be in those positions. If you inherit a situation like that, it will take time to filter through, weed out, and work in the faithful for those leadership positions. Then a pastor will save himself a lot of heartache, he won't be working up hill or won't be working with his hands tied behind his back. Therefore, it behooves the church to trust the leadership of the pastor as he urges for certain faithful people to be put into these key positions. The church is helping itself by going along with that.

Another thing about a faithful man is that he is loyal to his church, loyal to his pastor, wants to see his church progress, grow spiritually and grow in numbers. Obviously as more people come into the church changes may take place. Although the church may go through some changes, she must be willing for that to happen, as long as Scripture is not compromised. The faithful man loves his church, promotes his church, works in his church in some aspect or another and is not a "Lone Ranger" Christian type.

You may be fortunate enough to be called to pastor a church, which already has a group of faithful men. But if not, be not dismayed. Jesus started His ministry with a group of ragtag disciples. But God eventually used them to turn the world upside down!

"For ye see your calling, brethren, how that not many wise men after the flesh, not many mighty, not many noble, are called: But God hath chosen the foolish things of the world to confound the wise; and God hath chosen the weak things of the world to confound the things which are mighty; And base things of the world, and things which are despised, hath God chosen, yea, and things which are not, to bring to nought things that are: That no flesh should glory in his presence." (I Corinthians 1:26-29).

Who sets the agenda in the church? The pastor and the faithful men can better set the agenda of the church, rather than the agenda being set by the whim or opinion of some spiritually immature person. Here we are talking about true leadership—the leadership of the Holy Spirit. So as we see, as the pastor listens to the counsel of godly faithful men, he is not being a dictator. He is absorbing the voice of God from many sources and putting it all together; which should be part of the gift of being a pastor—that is, being able to hear the sheep and know what the needs of the sheep are. He would also be able to listen to brothers and sisters in Christ. "Iron sharpeneth iron; so a man sharpeneth the countenance of his friend." (Proverbs 27:17). Being able to organize that information, being able to administrate that information, being able to interpret that information, being able to apply that information, should all be involved in the pastor's gifts and callings that he has from the Lord.

Many good ideas may come forth; however, they can't all be implemented at once or in a certain way. God will give the pastor wisdom in filtering through ideas, and even words of the Lord from people. We don't want to go running off on one word and make it the ultimate mandate. Rather, we want to keep the person of Christ to be central: the whole character of Christ—not just one aspect of His character. The whole ministry—not just one aspect of ministry—keeping focused on Jesus—so as to not have another gospel, but the gospel of the Lord Jesus Christ.

14

The Pastor is the Church's Champion

In Acts 4:17 the disciples were asked by what authority they did these things. They let it be known that it was not by man's authority but by the authority of the Lord Jesus Christ and of His name. There are many pastors these days who feel whipped, brow beaten, stepped on and used. They feel like puppets. They feel like they are a front for other people's agendas, the whipping boys. And many of these pastors go around with their heads down. They have lost their joy, their strength, their power and their testimony. Some of them get out of the ministry. Some of them just do nothing but coast, are stagnate, and blame other people for their condition. They've forgotten this passage that we just read in Acts, "by what authority do you do these things." (Acts 4:17)

The pastor should be the champion for the local church. He should stand tall with his head high, with a smile on his face, with a vision in his eye, with a sword in his hand, with one knee bowed to the King of Kings and the Lord of Lords, with a spring in his step—not being beaten down, whipped by pawns of Satan who like to discourage men in the ministry. The pastor should not put down his shield of faith but hold it up high. Jesus was beaten, whipped, scourged, criticized, misunderstood, spit upon, despised, mocked, and rejected by men. But He kept His eyes on the Heavenly Father and kept about the task. Jesus never lost His joy! It's true He lost His life, but even in the losing of His life, He accomplished the perfect will of the Heavenly Father. And three days later He rose from the dead! It doesn't matter about outward circumstances; it doesn't matter about whether the people are following or not following, or listening or not listening. Jesus was able to powerfully preach the truth even to a room full of Pharisees!

The pastor is like the watchman on the wall who sounds the warning. Hallelujah, we need some men of God! We need some men who will stand no matter what, even if no one else stands. We need some men who will not let the whims of the congregation, the feeling of the moment, his own anxieties, doubt, or discouragements get him down. We live in a day and age where the church needs some strong leaders, men who aren't wimpy, sissy, or pansies. We don't need men who always wear their feelings on their sleeve, always need stroked, being patted by the congregation or someone else. We need men who are willing to grit their teeth and go on with God, no matter if anybody appreciates them or ever thanks them, men who are serving the Master, who aren't serving their own career goals, or money, or popularity or anything else.

Our churches need pastors who have solid Biblical convictions and will stand for their convictions; who aren't easily swayed or influenced by the whims of the times or popular teachings of the day—even though those popular teachings may be by very prominent men in religious circles, who have great followings. Large numbers of the congregation may even like such popular teaching. If those teachings are straying from Scripture, then it's like when Paul wrote to the Galatians and warned them, "Who hath bewitched you, oh foolish Galatians, that you began with such simplicity in Christ, but now you are following after (in their case) the popular teaching of legalism." (Gal. 3:1)

Pastor, you need to know how to stand for what is right without putting down the individual liberty of conscience that another person may have. Every person is entitled to his own personal convictions; however, that person's convictions should not set the agenda for the whole church. Scripture sets the agenda; there is not another gospel; and there is only one gospel. Part of the pastor's task is to keep the church's focus on the one gospel, not to be side tracked by minor issues. Even if those minor issues are sometimes true. (For example, chewing gum, hairstyles, trick or treating, diets, home schooling, etc.).

Pastors should major on the major, and minor on the minor. Jesus is the major, the person of Christ. We need pastors to stand up for Scriptural principles. This covers everything from church membership, who's allowed into your church, to all other things and practices in church. If you think about who is allowed into the church of Jesus Christ, who becomes a part of the Body of Christ, it is that person who names the name of Jesus Christ as personal Savior. That's it. No works, no doctrines, no resume has to be given, no perfect life has to be offered, simple faith in Christ gets you into the body of Christ. Acts 2:47 (NIV) "And the Lord added to their number daily those who were being saved."

Why should a local church have higher standards to get into its body, than Jesus has to get into His Kingdom? If Jesus accepts that person, then the church should accept that person. That does not mean that the church approves everything that person does or believes. Hopefully by coming into the church they will be in Sunday school classes, sit under preaching and teaching and guidance from the church to lead them out of any heresy they may practice or believe. The main thing is Jesus, and the pastor has to stand on the main thing. Some people in the church may not like it if some people come in dressed differently than they do. It doesn't matter. They may believe differently on certain issues than others do, it doesn't matter. Or they may have different spiritual gifts. The pastor is to stand strong, be a defender of the faith, the faith in Jesus Christ.

Some people might object to such an open door policy in the church; they say it is watering down the gospel. Oh no, that is the gospel! The gospel is that the poor, the needy, those bound by Satan can be helped. You do not put clean clothes into the washing machine; the washing machine is for dirty clothes. Church is a hospital for sinners not a showcase for saints. Let them in. That doesn't mean you put spiritually immature people in a position of leadership, (see the chapter on "Faithful Men"), but they have to be connected to the body to start receiving the life giving blood flow of the Lord Jesus Christ!

Another way to look at this is like when you bring a little baby home from the hospital. The baby has no conception of what that home stands for, of what lies ahead, what mommy and daddy believe. All that baby has done is that it was born into that family and is accepted with wide-open arms into the home. That baby does some things like keeping mom and dad up at night crying and whining, burping, messing its diapers. However, the goal is for mom and dad to raise that child to the point where that child can understand the visions, goals and values of mom and dad. That's the same way in the church. Babies are born into the Kingdom of God; you don't wait for those babies to mature before you bring them into the church. There may be a lot of things they may not understand.

Scripture teaches we all must become as little children to get into the Kingdom of God. How much does a child understand about predestination or when the rapture occurs or the doctrine of the Trinity? A child understands very little, but I know when I was seven years old I prayed and asked Jesus into my heart. I know I became a Christian, and I became a part of the Body of Christ. I thank God they didn't wait until I was thirty three years old, later in life, and had a college degree, or gone to Bible college, or sat through thirteen Sunday school classes, or five membership sessions, or had arrived to perfection before they accepted me into the local body of believers! We're setting ourselves above God when we make our church requirements higher standards then the standards that God has for the people that come into His family. Since God has the highest standards, any standards a church has that differs with God's, are actually "lower" standards!

Folks, they have become a part of the family. It is a sin for a church to keep people out of their family because they don't have full understanding yet. The other side of the coin concerns people who are already in the church, and who are living in sin, and are bringing detriment to the cause of Christ. If they have been thoroughly taught that it is sin (and it is obvious sin, overt sin, it is common knowledge that it is sin), and have been properly warned according to Scripture (Matthew 18:17; I Corinthians 5:5, etc.), there comes a time to withdraw fellowship from that person.

So you see, one of the tasks of the pastor is to keep the church from becoming a social club or religious clique—a place where people gather because they have a lot in common. Folks, the only thing we need to have in common is the Lordship of Jesus Christ in our lives. "Praising God, and having favor with all the people. And the Lord added to the church daily such as should be saved."(Acts 2:47). Jesus is what we have in common, and the pastor needs to stand STRONG for Jesus! That is the beauty of the church: that people can love one another through the grace of God, in spite of differences. Rather than the pastor caving into special interest groups in the church, he is to stand for the liberty we have in Christ, the freedom we have in Christ, allowing every person to walk in the liberty that Christ has given them. Teach them to not impose their personal conscience on someone else, but to give the other person liberty and not try to play the Holy Spirit for the other person. Romans 14 teaches us to live by higher principles: don't judge and don't cause one to stumble, but love.

You have the freedom to worship God however He leads you to worship Him. In our church I tell the folks in the congregation that they have liberty of worship; however, just don't knock the person over who is standing next to you! In other words, we shouldn't let other people dampen our worship, but on the same token we don't need to interfere with their worship (if they want to stand up and raise their hands and wave their arms or whatever). We just need to be careful that we're not forcing ourselves on the person next to us. His style may be to sit there and worship very quietly, so grant him his freedom. But if you worship in a demonstrative manner, he may try to hinder your freedom.

He may say to you, "But what about the Scriptural injunction that says that in the church things are to be done decently and in order?" Man has lots of orders, and the Pharisees were real big about all of their orders that they had, but they didn't necessarily come from God. To do things decently and in order means to follow the leading of the Holy Spirit – of course, first of all adhering to the teachings of Scripture, and then following the Spirit's leading. The Spirit may lead you to worship in a very demonstrative way or perhaps a very calm way. The word "reverence" in the dictionary has nothing to do with being quiet. It has to do with obedience (the root meaning of reverence.) So we're to obey God in our life and particularly how we operate in church.

For instance, I have seen church services where people were very quiet, and the service was very solemn, and some people said that it was a very reverent atmosphere. However, if the people in that particular so-called reverent service were not totally surrendering to God and obeying God, then it was the most irreverent church service that there could be. And then on the other hand you may go into a church service that seems very loud and noisy. People may be moving around, and maybe, to man, it looks like disorder. But if God ordered it, and if those people are submissive to God, and obedient to God, they're being very reverent. "By this shall all men know that ye are my disciples, if you have love for one another." (John 13:35). Not "by this shall all men know that you are my disciples when all your doctrine is correct, or all your practices, programs, or traditional styles are correct."

When Peter told pastors to take the "oversight" of the flock (I Peter 5:2), he didn't say to merely "take a position." He meant, "discharge your duties." (Vines Dictionary of New Testament Words, p. 834). Be a champion for your flock!

Goliath was called the "champion" of the Philistines. But David, the shepherd, slew him. "When the Philistines saw their champion was dead,

89

they fled." (I Samuel 18:51). David was not a champion by watching from the sidelines, but by entering the fight.

Webster's Dictionary defines "champion" as "one who fights for another or for a cause." Jesus was the greatest champion who ever walked on the earth. Pastor, champion the cause of Christ in your church! Fight the devil and the Goliaths for your sheep!

15.

The Pastor is a Polished Arrow

Isaiah 49:1-6 (NIV) says, "Before I was born the Lord called me," even though you and I, pastor, didn't become aware of it until later on in our lives. "He made me into a polished arrow and concealed me in his quiver." This reminds me of the story from folklore that a silver bullet can kill a werewolf. We are God's special arrow or silver bullet that is set aside (perhaps even for the opportune moment) to be used to destroy the works of Satan.

"But I said, 'I have labored to no purpose; I have spent my strength in vain and for nothing. Yet what is due me is in the Lord's hand and my reward is with my God." That kind of speaks for itself. Sometimes when we get discouraged and we think we are not making any headway or progress, we are working in vain. God knows what we are doing and knows our reward. "It is too small a thing for you to be my servant to restore the tribes of Jacob. I will also make you a light or the Gentiles that you might bring my salvation to the ends of the earth." God has given us a larger vision than just the inside of the four walls of the church.

The devil knows you are a threat to his kingdom, so he will try to discourage you and tempt you to jump out of the quiver. But, my dear brother, it is an honor just to be in God's quiver! One of these days the Master Archer is going to need that special polished arrow. And He is going to reach into His quiver, pull you out, place you into His bow, draw the string and let you fly straight into the target He is aiming at! So stay available, stay in the Word and prayer, stay faithful in the little things; God's timing is perfect. The Hebrew word for "polished" is defined as: to make bright, choice, chosen, plumed, clearly polished, pure, purged. In English we hone an arrow, to sharpen or to smooth to exact specifications, with a honing stone containing abrasive material. Notice that for the arrow to become polished or honed you use abrasive material on it.

So when we come across church problems and difficult members, "Consider it pure joy, my brothers, whenever you face trials of many kinds, because you know that the testing of your faith develops perseverance." (James 1:2-3 NIV). Remember God's opinion of you. You have to keep your focus not on people but on Jesus. Also remember

God says you are a polished arrow and He is polishing you, honing you. Sometimes when you think that God has put you on a shelf, and you are not being used, and your gifts and your talents aren't being maximized, just remember it is an honor to be in the quiver.

That reminds me of the story of the little water faucet. It is not running all the time but just sitting there. What if that water faucet started becoming depressed and discouraged because it wasn't being used? On one occasion the owner walks by and hears the faucet crying, and says, "What's wrong?" The faucet answers, "I have a lot of water to give you, but here I sit idle and feeling useless." The point is, it's available to the owner, and the owner can come by any time and turn the tap and get water out of it. It is a privilege just to be an available servant. Here in this passage in Isaiah, Isaiah is called a servant. We know he is talking to the Jews at that moment; but he is also talking prophetically about the Lord Jesus Christ when He comes and He is the servant. Christ said in John 14:12 that I will do even greater works than He did. So we are the servants of the most High God. It is a privilege to be in God's quiver. PTL!

You don't have to be a success in the world's eyes or even in the eyes of popular Christianity. "Moreover it is required in stewards that a man be found faithful" (I Corinthians 4:2). I think of Jeremiah's ministry who appears not to have one convert, but he was faithful to the task and did what God asked him to do, even though he didn't have a great response from people. Now the other side of the coin is God doesn't want a person to be lazy and use this excuse to not ever lead a soul to Christ. The point is: are you attempting to lead souls to Christ? Are you setting appointments with lost people, are you seeking out lost people – "seeking and saving those which are lost"? (Luke 19:10).

The odds are some are going to be saved, although some may not be, like in Jeremiah's ministry. Rather than asking how many have you seen saved, ask how many people have you witnessed to? The church doesn't need a pastor who is lazy. The pastor doesn't have to be some flamboyant success by man's standards. On the other hand, he is to be a success in the eyes of God. He must be faithful and must be working, diligent, tending to the flock.

One secret to success in the ministry is to realize that you may not be a success, according to man's standard or in the world's eyes. Look not at the fact that you are not succeeding, but realize that the Lord is keeping track. See, Jesus was not a success in the world's eyes. He was a failure by most human standards. He had a small band of men. He was despised and rejected of men, had no place to lay His head. He was tried, convicted as a criminal, crucified, and denied even in His trial by His close friend Peter. He didn't' start a college, didn't write a book, just wandered around the countryside. Of course we know that in God's sight He was a complete success. Sometimes the fruit of our labor comes later. Makes sense that if you plant something you don't get fruit right away.

So as ministers, we need to understand this principle. Because if we don't, we will get to think that our success is based upon man's opinion of us. And then we will have a tendency to compromise, be men pleasers, tickle people's ears. We will have the tendency to be intimidated by a group of people inside the church or outside the church, who will tell us we will not be a success unless we meet their standards, their specifications, their desires. And we will be looking for their approval and a pat on the back rather than looking to please the most High God.

We will begin to even measure our own success by comparing ourselves with other ministers who maybe do have large crowds that follow them, or have books printed, or colleges started in their name. This could easily sidetrack us from our own calling over consideration of what others are doing and saying to us. When those come against us, we could assume that, "I am not a success, because people are against me." Or when we urge a program or ministry to start (and it never gets off the ground), we then try to measure our success by that. Or when we lose some faithful followers, we could assume that we are a failure.

Jesus was not a failure! Jesus was a complete success. He lost every one of the twelve disciples at some point. One of them even went and committed suicide after he had betrayed Him. There will be people in your ministry who will betray you. There will be modern day Judases along the way. There will be others who try to give you "good" advice. Peter was always sticking his foot in his mouth, even giving Jesus wrong counsel. If we aren't careful, we will be looking in the wrong places for a measure of success. God is looking for someone who is a polished arrow, who is in the quiver and available and waiting to be used by Him. That is

93

one of the keys to success in the ministry. This affects our attitude. It's been said your attitude determines your altitude. If you want to fly high as a minister, it has nothing to do with how many showed up for church on Sunday, or how many people appreciated your sermon. If before God you can be open and honest and transparent and be able to say to the Lord," I am doing your will," then frankly it doesn't matter how man may respond.

Now I admit that's nice when man responds in a positive manner to your ministry. If you have this correct attitude, it will keep you from getting discouraged in your ministry. It will keep you from getting depressed, defeated, frustrated, and angry. I don't think that the polished arrow in the quiver is frustrated. Of course, neither is a dead man, (I talked about that earlier in the book). So, it is very important that we understand this principle. Then you can minister with excitement and with joy. Although what is happening around you may not look exciting to anybody, but you know you are walking in God's will, then that is exciting! "But they that wait upon the Lord shall renew their strength; they shall mount up with wings as eagles; they shall run, and not be weary; and they shall walk, and not faint." (Isaiah 40:31).

16

The Pastor Guides the Church

The pastor should often bring to light the direction, the vision, the goals, and statements that we are one in Christ. State what unity is based around; reminding the people not to get unnerved when the attacks of Satan come. The devil does attack when you are on the right road. Put to rest, in other words, negative reactions and thoughts. Squelch accusations that if anything at all is not quite right in the church we must be doing something wrong.

The pastor should constantly assure the people that the way he is leading and the way the church is going is right (if indeed it is). Inform them that attacks are to be expected. Remind the people that we are one. Remind them of their identity in Christ. Remind the church of its identity, and that it is going forward, and will not be judged by outward appearance; God looks on the heart. The church members often need reassurances that they are on the right track.

The pastor should allow other people to operate, to minister, and to fulfill their spiritual gifts. The pastor shouldn't get off track of what his main calling is. In fact, it could be something as simple as the church is dirty and no one's cleaning it, then the pastor goes and cleans it. No, don't do that. If the people see that the pastor is not going to do it, then someone may arise and do it or hire a janitor. The pastor doesn't have to have his finger in every pie, controlling everything or micro-managing. He should be able to release people and free people up to use their liberty and their gifts and callings. He should only step in if the overall purpose needs some guidance or is being violated by someone. But don't try to do everything. People should know, if they are given the liberty to lead, that the pastor isn't going to tell them what to do. The pastor should encourage them, be their cheerleader.

Also remind the folks that the church is the church of the Lord Jesus Christ. It doesn't belong to man; the head of the church is Jesus not man. It rests upon Christ and His power to even get good deeds done in the church, not our good deeds but Him doing the good deeds through us. The church needs to rest in Him. It is His church and the problems that come up are His problems. On more than one occasion, when I have faced problems in the church, I have prayed, "God, you have a problem to solve – it's <u>YOUR</u> church not <u>MINE</u>!" Take the problems to Him. They are opportunities for Him to work. Sometimes we get overwhelmed with situations, but it's not so bad to be brought down to our knees (a great place to be!) and cry out to the Lord for answers, for guidance and for direction.

Another way to look at problems is perhaps it is a problem of being too sentimental. Maybe sister so and so has been playing the organ for 20 years, but the music is dead and getting nowhere. The church realizes this and knows God wants to make a change. A lot of people feel badly about removing her from that position or asking her to step down, thinking that would hurt her feelings (or if her family is involved in the church, hurt all of their feelings) since she has been organist for so long.

Of course, this must be handled carefully and with much love. But Jesus taught the principle that if the tree doesn't bear fruit cut it down. If someone is not producing fruit, it is time for that person to be replaced, or step down, or get into some other ministry. Perhaps they aren't even operating in their correct gift; or if that is their gift, they may be lazy and not working it. Somebody needs to be in it that can. Don't be too sentimental to the point of putting sentiment above what is right in the Kingdom of God and getting the job done.

The pastor should teach the folks the difference between conviction and an opinion, or a philosophy, or a tradition. If it really is black and white in the Scripture, it is a principle. Teach the people within the church to accept one another based on basic unity in Christ, not on agreement with specific legalistic practices.

One of the callings that God has put on my life is to be a herald of the liberty that we have in Jesus Christ, that we are not bound by man's traditions. We are to worship Jesus Christ, and not to make an idol of tradition. Quite frankly, it doesn't matter what that tradition is. How do you know if you are placing a tradition above Christ? You get bent out of shape with another Christian because he doesn't want your tradition. This comes from a lack of love and results in anger. Does it cool off your worship? Less love for church? Less fellowship? If a tradition takes supremacy over the lordship of Christ, that tradition has become an idol, a sacred cow, if you please.

For instance: the order of service, how we practice doing certain things in the church even though we have done it that way for one hundred years. I believe the seven last words of a dying church gasping its final breath are "We've never done it that way before." I have seen a multitude of churches in my life that are stagnant, not growing, and not shining lights for Christ. Although there are decent members in the church, they are making no impact on their own people, let alone on the community around them, because they are bound and determined to hold to man's traditions above the lordship of Christ and the free movement of His Holy Spirit. This means that sometimes there has to be change, because the Holy Spirit is not stagnant. As each year goes by, culture changes, and the gospel must be given in a relevant manner. The message never changes, but the method may have to change. Many times man makes a god out of the method. Paul says, "I am made all things to all men that I might by all means save some." (I Corinthians 9:22). To a Jew I must become a Jew, to a Gentile a Gentile, to a Greek a Greek. But sometimes churches may get stuck in a rut of tradition. One definition of a rut is a grave with both ends knocked out. I am not saying that having a tradition is wrong. I'm saying that when we let that tradition get in the way of our going on with God (because we don't want to change and we aren't comfortable with that change) then we have made a god out of that tradition. And we place more value on it than the fresh moving of God in our midst.

I have encountered some opposition to change in all of my pastorates. It's human nature to want to get one's way and to be comfortable. I believe that God calls pastors to comfort the afflicted and to afflict the comfortable. "Preach the word; be diligent in season, and out of season; reprove, rebuke, exhort with all long-suffering and doctrine." (II Timothy 4:2). That is where a lot of preachers get into trouble. There are people in churches that call a pastor just to tickle their ears. "For the time will come when they will not endure sound doctrine but, after their own lusts, shall they heap to themselves teachers, having itching ears." (II Timothy 4:3). They like the pastor to preach against alcoholics and drug addicts. But when the pastor preaches against their pet sin, pet wrong attitude, pet doctrine, or tradition, then their feathers get ruffled. Then they think that the preacher has gone to meddling instead of preaching, because you have touched their "idol." "These are rebellious people, deceitful children, and children unwilling to listen to the Lord's instruction. They say to the seers, 'See no more visions!' and to the prophets, 'Give us no more visions of what is right! Tell us pleasant things, prophesy illusions.'" (Isaiah 30:9-10 NIV).

After all, often just about the time a preacher is getting down to the bottom line of an area of the church where growth needs to take place, where the Lord needs to move in a fresh way, it scares some people to death. They are afraid that God is going to do something that they have never seen Him do. Many Christians are afraid of the Holy Spirit, and they are afraid of change. It might require them to change. (Change either their ways of doing church or change their preconceived doctrinal ideas.) Then rather than them do that, it's easier for them to say "Pastor we think your time is up here. Why don't you move on down the road?" If someone asks you to do this, say, "It's easier for you to move your membership than for me to move my family!"

I challenge everyone who says he is called to pastor a church, to stick with the church until God calls him elsewhere, and not let man call him away. I learned this through the godly counsel that I got from a dear pastor friend of mine, James Moore. I was seeking his counsel along this line on an occasion where some traditionalists were threatening me in our church. He said that he told his church that God had called him there, and that God would be the one to call him away. He wouldn't step down from that pulpit just because someone wanted him to. They would have to drive him away, and he would be clinging onto the pulpit, and screaming all the way to the back door the message that God had given him. He also told me, "Roger, God gave you the vision; don't let man dissuade you."

Too many times pastors tuck tail and run when they should stand and fight the wiles of the devil who would like to destroy our churches (not by overt sin but by subtlety), by not being willing to change in areas where God is saying they need to be changed. Many times in my life I've seen people who were supposed to be godly leaders in the church dig their heels in and turn a stubborn heart and deaf ear to the Spirit of the Living God. Some of those people have actually said to me, "Pastor, I don't care what the Bible says, we've never done it that way before," or "I've never experienced that." It makes me wonder why they ever called a pastor. I'll tell you why some churches call a pastor. They want him to entertain them on Sundays; they want a man to marry their children, bury their dead, and visit the sick in the hospital. They want a man to go through the outward rituals of what a pastor ought to do. But when it comes to actually shepherding, that is, giving guidance and leadership to the flock, they don't want that.

Not only is change difficult for many Christians, but also giving up control. They like the way that the flock is going. Many of them like the control they have, and they want to be the one that controls the flock. I thank God for pastors who believe God and hang in there until the leadership of the flock is transferred over to the rightful master—and that is Jesus Christ Himself who is the Lord of the church—not some group who may call themselves deacons or elders or whatever. In America today there is a spirit of rebellion against authority.

Not only is resistance to authority one of the undermining factors that is damaging our churches, but another thing is ignorance. "My people are destroyed for lack of knowledge; because thou hast rejected knowledge, I will also reject thee, that thou shalt be no priest to me; seeing thou hast forgotten the law of thy God, I will also forget thy children." (Hosea 4:6). The Pharisees were ignorant; they could quote Scriptures, but they did not understand God's heart. God said that Israel knew God's acts, but Moses knew God's ways (Psalm 103:7). It is time for the church to wake up and see God's ways—not just His acts, and how He did it in the past. God wants to act today and to make it known that Jesus is the Lord, and that Jesus is the boss of the church, not any man or group of men.

There is no such thing as seniority in the body of Christ and the church. Just because someone is a member longer than another doesn't mean he is more spiritual. (I Corinthians 3:1-3). Phariseeism has swept through the church like a wild fire! We tend, in our churches, to look down our pious noses at some brother who has been overtaken by booze or drugs. We can't see that the sin that Jesus attacked the most was that of phariseeism, judging, and legalism We tend to judge others who are not a clone of us. Pharisees follow the letter of the law and not the spirit of the law. "Who also hath made us able ministers of the new testament, not of the letter, but of the spirit; for the letter killeth, but the Spirit giveth life." (II Corinthians 3:6).

17.

Lessons from Timothy

I Timothy 3:14 (NIV) "I'm writing these instructions (same word 'instruction' in 1:18) so that if I'm delayed you will know how people ought to conduct themselves in God's household." This is so the pastor will know how Christians are supposed to act within the church—not necessarily within the four walls of the church but in the church body itself.

I Timothy 4:6 (NIV) "If you point these things out to the brothers," another job of a pastor is to point things out to the church and bring it to their attention. If you do that, "you'll be a good minister of Jesus Christ." There's that word 'good' again, the 'good' fight, and here's a 'good' minister of Jesus Christ.

I Timothy 4:7 (NIV) goes back to what I had previously mentioned: "Have nothing to do with godless myths and old wives tales, rather train yourself to be godly." This thing of fables and godless myths has to do with profane, meaning heathen and wicked. Teaching should have God in it, and not God out of it; thus, teaching a myth that is not Scriptural is actually wicked and heathen. Be careful about taking Scripture out of context. Old wives tales means "silly" in the Greek.

The same is in I Timothy 1:4 (NIV) "Don't have anything to do with godless myths, rather train yourself to be godly." So, the other side of the coin is rather than teaching doctrines and teachings that are godless, they should be godly. The pastor should be training himself to be godly, getting back to 1:18 where I had commented on instructing pastors so that they can fight the good fight of faith. The fighter gets training, and the training can come from his own discipline of exercises and also from the mentoring he can get from an actual trainer. Paul says to Timothy, "to train yourself to be godly." Training is very important. You are not training to box physically, but you are training to be godly. He is letting you know he is not talking about a physical training.

I Timothy 4:8 "For physical training is of some value, but godliness has value for all things, holding promise for both the present life and the life to

100

come." This particular godliness applies to godly teaching, rightly dividing the word of truth, not taking Scripture out of context.

In I Timothy 4:11 Paul says to Timothy, "Command and teach these things." There is a twofold task of the pastor, one is to give commands, referring back to what I said previously about the pastor standing strong, fighting the good fight, not being a wimp, to take a stand, to actually command (meaning, over my dead body will heresy be allowed to be presented in this church!), so command these things. And secondly, teach these things.

Verse 12, "Don't let anyone look down on you because you're young." In other words, there are outward things people may look at; like your age, status, wealth, education, or lack of experience. But just because you're young in age doesn't mean you're young in the Lord and maturity necessarily. So one way that you can help prevent people from looking down on you is by setting an example for the believers in speech, life, love, faith, and purity—so you don't come across as some little, young, fresh out of Bible college student, know it all, still wet behind the ears, prideful or more spiritual person than everybody else. Your walk must back up your talk.

So set an example, and then it's not as likely people would look down on you because of your age. Is there a real maturity in your walk, not in your physical years? Set an example for the believers in speech. It is in how you talk, and what you say, and in the spirit in which you say it, and also in your life (the Christlike life) and in love. The Bible says speak the truth in love and in faith (Ephesians 4:15). We tell people to walk by faith; are we walking by faith? And then an example in purity: that is a life that portrays the holiness that we have in Christ, so that holiness that is on the inside works its way to the outside.

Verse 13, "until I come devote yourself to the public reading of Scripture, to preaching and to teaching." It's one thing to read Scripture in our private devotions, but we should share Scripture in public. In fact, the basis of the sermon should be from Scripture. And the Scripture should be read, because what we're preaching is based on Scripture. So go ahead and read that Scripture that you are preaching about. I don't think this is only applying to the formal sermon, but occasionally in church Scriptures are to be read even if you don't comment on them.

101

Verse 14, "Do not neglect your gift which was given to you through a prophetic message when the body of elders laid their hands on you." In other words, Timothy had certain giftings and that gift was to be used. He was to operate in his spiritual gift and not neglect it. It would behoove a pastor to find out how he has been gifted by the Holy Spirit and operate in that. As you operate in your gift you will find the most fulfillment. If you try to get outside of your gift (even though you are doing nice things) you will find great frustration.

So operate within your gifts. The Bible says neglect not your gift. There is a unique calling that God puts on ministers and pastors in different ways and in different forms of operation. What the minister does, and how he approaches pastoring and presenting the gospel, is to be done in that gift where God has given him that strength. Sometimes I hear people talk about, "Well, a chain is only as strong as its weakest link," as if you have to try to make up for the gifts that you don't have. This is where other church members and their gifts can operate.

Since we're looking at this, the body of Christ is a team effort with various parts, the body, the foot, the hand and the eye. If your gift is in, let's say, evangelism, you might get very frustrated trying to pastor and deal with the ins and outs of everyday decisions within the church. And on the other hand, if your gift is pastoring, and all you're doing is evangelism and winning souls, your heart's going to be torn because you can't stay with those souls and help disciple them.

For example, on a basketball team some guys are gifted at the three-point shot—don't put them underneath the basket, but feed it to them on the outside and let them operate in their gift and let them make the three-point shots. Some guys work better under the basket, so funnel the ball into them so they can dunk the ball and do their layups or whatever. You put them on the outside perimeter shooting, and their weakness shows up. It is possible, obviously, to neglect your gift as a pastor—where then you actually become a square peg in a round hole.

God made us, and when He calls us He gives us the tools and the resources that we need to do the job He wants us to do. The pastor should determine what God has actually called him to do specifically and how God wants him to go about it in his own unique way as God has gifted him. This also keeps us from looking down on or judging others who don't do it just like we do it. They are gifted perhaps in different ways than we are, and their emphasis will be different according to their giftings.

I Timothy 4:5, "Be diligent in these matters". "Diligent" means stick to it, do it, give yourself wholly to them, not halfhearted, and not just a little dab, not one foot in and one foot out, and be fully committed to the ministry that God has called you to—so that everyone may see your progress. In other words, as people rub shoulders with you they should be able to see that your walk with Christ is a mature walk.

Verse 16, "Watch your life and doctrine closely. Persevere in them, because if you do, you will save both yourself and your hearers." You don't want your own life to be disqualified. Paul said, "When I have preached to others, I myself might be a castaway." (I Corinthians 9:27). You want your own testimony and influence to remain intact. You want your hearers not to be led astray by your lack of diligence or your lack of perseverance.

I heard someone say that they've never seen so many weak-kneed Christians as they see in America today. Meaning: halfhearted, give up so easily, get discouraged so easily, whine so easily, throw in the towel so easily, lose their temper, get mad at the church, get mad so easily at people they are ministering to.   Thank God, Jesus didn't do this! Because what if you had someone like Peter in your church, and he maintained to your face, "not so Lord," as he said to Jesus? Peter was pretty flaky at times, but Jesus did not get discouraged. Jesus persevered. So the pastor, it is saying here, must persevere especially in these matters that he had just talked about: of walking by faith and with a good example in faith, love, and purity.

Another example of not letting anyone look down upon you because you're young is in I Timothy 5. How does the young pastor approach an older Christian?   "Do not rebuke an older man." And that word "rebuke" in the Greek is different from some of the other words "rebuke", because the Bible says reprove, rebuke, exhort. We are to rebuke everyone. But this kind of rebuking is like when I grew up in the South we had a saying "to light into", to really get in somebody's face. In the King James the word is simply "rebuke"; but NIV says, "Don't rebuke an older man <u>harshly</u>". The NIV elaborates a little more on the actual meaning of this particular Greek word for rebuke. That meant "to come down on". You're to approach an older man with more respect. In fact, it says exhort him as if he were your father.

The pastor in chapter 5:1 is to "treat the younger men as brothers." It's talking about our relationship. Treat the older women as mothers and the younger women as sisters with absolute purity. This should help pastors not yield to sexual temptation with younger women. You wouldn't want to have sex with your sister, so deal with the younger women as you would with your actual sister. Yes, they are female, but your relationship to them is not male and female. Treat the younger women as sisters like you would love your sister with care. See how the church is a <u>family</u>. It is <u>not</u> a <u>business</u>! The pastor should seek to guide the church as a family, and not as an institution or organization or a business.

I get tired of hearing the pastor is a professional and he should act in a professional manner in the ministry. I'm sure there's a good side to that, but so often I see where pastors tend to be a little aloof, a little bit better than others. They keep people at arm's length. They don't get involved in the lives of people, in the lives of the flock. Well, we don't do that to our father or our mother or sister or brother—which is exactly what Paul is telling Timothy to do here—to treat them like family members. There is that warmth and caring. There is not some cold, formal approach of the minister pastor sitting up in his ivory tower with his holy robes on, as if he has to portray some kind of air, some kind of an image, that he is the "pastor".

In fact, what Paul had just told Timothy is so that people can see your walk with God. If you want to portray something that is what you want to portray—your love for the Lord Jesus Christ, your obedience to Him. Not some preconceived idea of how a pastor is suppose to dress, how he is supposed to act, and so forth, like he never can let his hair down. Don't you let your hair down with your family? Be real! Don't be a phony baloney. Don't be stuck up. Don't put up a wall around you.

Be open. Be transparent. Because if people think that you are real, then they feel there is hope for them too. Many times they will think the pastor can't identify with them, because they think he is somewhat separate (in the sense that he doesn't have a real life.) I wonder sometimes how they think the pastor ever has children (as if he never even had sex with his wife). I tell men that when I get up in the morning, I put my britches on one leg at a time, just like they do. Do some studies in other Scriptures, rather than just right here, of how you are supposed to treat a father, mother, sister, and brother—that will give the pastor some hints of how people can relate to him as pastor and how he can relate to them.

You want people to be able to relate to you. You deal with life issues also. They need to know that you are a real person, that you have hurts, pains, sorrows, trials, and joys just like they do. You're trying to set an example of how you get through it. They need to see your leaning on Christ is the same way they can get through it. Part of your instruction to them is your actual life itself, plus how you approach them; because how you approach them tells a whole lot about how they may receive you and receive what you have to say.

The word "instruction" shows up again in I Timothy 5:7 "Give the people these instructions, too, so that no one may be open to blame." The pastor doesn't want people in his flock to be open to fault. One way to help people not to be opened to blame is to give them proper instruction. And so, the pastor should ask himself, if he finds out that his members of his flock are not living the Christian life that they should, (in this particular case taking care of the widows and providing for your own family): "Has the pastor taught on this? Has he lived this example in front of them? Has he gotten this truth across?" It is true that you may teach and preach it, but that doesn't mean that people receive it. You do have to ask yourself the question, "Have I given clear instruction?"

So any areas where you find fault in the church, pastor, ask yourself these questions: "Have I given instruction on how to avoid this fault? Have I covered this, not only from the pulpit, but one-on-one with this person, through the ministry of the church, or through the elders, deacons or teachers that are in the church? Have they received the discipling they need? Or is it that they have received it, heard it, or been shown it in word and in deed, but they just have been rebellious and refuse to heed it?"

On the subject of training and discipling new Christians, I often overlooked what the Great Commission was really saying. I thought it was saying "teach them my commandments", but actually He is saying to teach them to <u>obey</u> everything I have commanded you. To train somebody doesn't mean that you just fill their head with information, or facts, or memorization of Bible verses, as good as that may be. To train is almost like instinct, like when I was in the army and I was trained how to respond. You don't have to think about it. It almost comes natural. In other words, living the Christian life as Christ would becomes natural, as we just walk in obedience. Obedience becomes the natural thing.

To train somebody to deal with a trial in life, you walk through the trial together with him. To train somebody about evangelism you take that person with you, let him observe you evangelizing, and let him have some turns of evangelizing—not just giving them a book on how to win souls or tell them the facts about it. To train them about marriage live a good, godly, dynamic marriage in front of that person. That will give them training on how to have a good marriage, not just a bunch of theories and facts about it. To really teach means that they grasp it so they can start obeying. And when they are on their own, and the teacher is not there, they have been trained to obey.

"Thank you, Lord, for giving us lessons from Timothy so we aren't left to fend for ourselves."

18.

Plain Ole Jesus

Mark 2:1-2 is the occasion when Jesus was preaching in the house. They came not for a big healing campaign or miracle service. Jesus was in the house, plain ole Jesus preaching in the house. People did end up getting healed, but the house was filled with people. I believe that as people hear that Jesus is in the house, that Jesus is in our lives, that Jesus is in our church meetings, people will come—because they know Jesus is there. We don't need to denigrate plain ole Jesus. What has become wrong today in American churches with just having plain ole Jesus? What has happened to Christians who go looking for every new thing? They are looking for the show, the hype, and the manifestations. What we need is plain ole Jesus.

Peter and John said, "Silver and gold have I none but such as I have give I thee." (Acts 3:6). All they had was Jesus! So that's what the church needs—just Jesus! They can have other stuff, but just make sure in among all the stuff we are offering Jesus. That applies in everything we do. Where is Jesus—plain ole Jesus—in every ministry we have? Quite frankly, if our ministries don't have Jesus in it, it's of no avail. It's just what man can do. That would include any seminary class that is taught, any Bible college class, any Sunday school class, any ministry in the church including any benevolence ministry, children's ministry, youth ministry, visitation ministry, or whatever we're doing—including this book! Where is Jesus in all of this? Where is Jesus in our Bible studies, or are we just reading the Bible to be academically smarter and more informed? Jesus should be in every aspect, every fiber of our being, and in every minute of every day.

Paul said, "Pray without ceasing" (I Thessalonians 5:17)—our focus needs to be constantly on Jesus. He is the one motivating us, leading us, guiding us, moving in and through us. It's our walk—we are walking in the Spirit. So where is Jesus in all our religious activities? I think of all the various para-church ministries that go on today. There is nothing wrong with para-church ministries. But the question we need to ask is "Where is Jesus in this?" If a para-church ministry is really effective in advancing the Kingdom, it is because they are putting plain ole Jesus in the center of their ministry. So if you think about it that way, you can, my dear friend, accomplish what God wants you to accomplish. (Of course, He is doing it <u>through</u> you).

If you have plain ole Jesus in the midst of what you're doing, it's not like you have to travel all around the world to go to some special conference somewhere to gather some kind of secret information that only that conference has and only that teacher can offer. You have Jesus, and when you have Jesus you have it all! Understand, of course, that I'm not leaving out the Father or the Spirit, for in Christ dwells the fullness of the Godhead bodily. (Colossians 2:9).

Thousands of new teachings have come down the line, (I can list hundreds just since I've been in the ministry): of this conference, that style of evangelism, this style of preaching, that church's method, this methodology of reaching our world, how to be salt, how to be light, and the latest everything. For example, I had never heard the phrase "World View"(W.V.) until recently in my life. I got to looking into it – it's a great thing. They are teaching people to have a correct W. V. There are even W.V Conferences. Every time Peter, Paul, or James or any of the disciples preached, they were presenting the correct W.V. So there has been a W.V. all along without a W.V. Conference. If you just get in the Word of God, and walk in the Spirit of God, and believe what the Bible says, you have the correct W.V. It is nothing new. Ecclesiastes says, "There is nothing new under the sun." When will the church of Jesus Christ, the Christians wake up and realize all you need is Jesus? Because if you're walking in obedience to Jesus, and walking in the Spirit, and allowing Him to live His life through you, you do have the correct W.V. You will be walking in power and authority. And it all comes from Jesus. That way Jesus gets the glory and the credit, not some man or organization and not some so called, "new teaching" that is out there. If it is good teaching, it came from the Bible. So let's not get hung up on labels and men and methods, but realize behind it all is Jesus.

I think of Evangelism Explosion(E.E.)—that blessed me greatly. I went through the E.E. material, but when you boiled it down, it was plain ole Jesus. They had an E.E. in the book of Acts. It's a way, I guess, of packaging. Don't think if you don't have the package, you can't have the real deal. There are a lot of things today that are packaged pretty, but they may be empty. So don't get to thinking you can't have it, and you can't evangelize because you hadn't attended an E.E. conference, or you can't have a W.V. because you haven't attended a W.V. conference, or you can't have a good marriage because you hadn't attended a marriage conference, or you can't be salt and light because you hadn't attended a salt and light conference.

The Bible says the disciples turned the world upside down. They were salt and light. They didn't have some of the things we have today as far as resources. There's a good point. You see, our greatest resource is God himself. Our greatest resource is the Word of God, the Holy Spirit residing in us, the person of Jesus Christ who lives in us. As Paul said, "I can do all things through Christ who strengthens me." We may think, "Well, I don't have the resources." It has nothing to do with money or buildings, or education. It has nothing to do with many of the trappings and the supplements that are offered.

For instance, if you're eating correct food and good food, you don't need any supplements. Just like where I live out in rural Kansas, the ranchers, during the winter time as they feed their cattle hay, will also add rations (supplements) to the cattle's food. The cow is in the lot or pen and eating the meager fare of last season's hay, but the cow needs more. If the cow is eating good, fresh grass in the summer pasture, the cow is getting what it needs.

It's the same way with people taking vitamins, and that's OK, if you don't think you are eating a good healthy diet. But maybe because of your schedule, or maybe because you are not close to a natural food source, you need supplements. But isn't it a sorry state of affairs when the church of the Lord Jesus Christ is not offering basic good food, and people have to go and get supplements somewhere else!

Think about it: would there be a need for para-church ministries (operating independently of and with no connection to local churches) if the church was doing what it was supposed to? Would there be a need for people to go running around away from their church to have to get supplemental feedings? May God grant that we as pastors and as churches would be offering well balanced, nutritional, spiritual meals to people, so there would be no such need. I thank God for supplements; as I said sometimes you aren't able to get the nutrition wherever. The bottom line is in Christ. He is sufficient! The Bible says, "My grace is sufficient for you." Jesus is all we need. But sometimes the church is not presenting that as it should and as it could. I'm saying it could if the church would rely on Jesus. Thank God somebody, like para-church ministries, is doing it and picking up the slack where the church has left off. Jesus died for the church—not the para-church. If the church would realize the resources that the church has in Christ, the church would be a lot more effective and see a lot more ministries get done in the community and across the world.

As you think about the importance of the church, I think sometimes we have pooh-poohed the church as though it is inadequate in and of itself as an entity. But as you read the New Testament, the Bible says that God has gifted the church. In the church are represented various spiritual gifts. But sometimes gifted people are not operating in church because the church doesn't recognize their gift or won't allow them to operate.

I'm not talking about operating just within the four walls of a building. The church could even send its members out, as the church in Antioch sent out missionaries. Read the book of Acts. You show me in the book of Acts any para-church ministry or any mission organization not connected to a church. The church is the body of Christ. As the body functions according to the strengths and resources that it has in Christ, we too would be able to turn our world upside down. So let's get back to the basics here and stand up and be who we are in Christ, not only as individuals but as a church!

I'm reminded of what Jesus said to the disciples when He fed the 5,000, "You feed them." The disciples said, "All we have are two small fish and five loaves of bread." Isn't that interesting? He didn't say, "Go find someone else to feed them, go raise funds somewhere and see if you can come up with what is needed, send out letters." He said, "You feed them." They found out that they could as they used whatever resources they had. The bottom line is when Jesus blessed the five loaves and two fish that they had, they ended up feeding the 5,000. The church should not take a back seat! The church should be the cutting edge. The church should be the forerunner, the front runner blazing the trail. It's a sad day in the history of the church when you have people having to go outside of the church to blaze the trail. I thank God for those churches who do reach out. But for whatever reason at some point the church is not doing it, I am glad that other ministries step up to the plate and make up the difference.

What I am saying is let's emphasize and practice true Biblical Christianity and true New Testament Church!

What about some of the preachers that you see on TV? Some of them have wild and strange doctrines. It's like they are trying to teach some kind of a new revelation that you've never heard of before. I Timothy 1:4-5 (NIV) talks about this, "They devote themselves to myths and endless genealogies. They promote controversies rather than God's work. The goal of this command is love which comes from a pure heart and a good conscience and sincere faith." You see, the goal of teaching right doctrine is not to espouse some fancy scheme or some mystery that you discovered by reading between the lines in the Bible. But the goal is always love and good works. Otherwise, knowledge "puffeth up" (I Corinthians 8:1). And that stems from pride, pride that somebody knows something that somebody else doesn't know. Some "new thing" or a "deeper thing" that they have "supposedly" discovered. Jesus is enough!

I Timothy 1:6-7, "Some have wandered away from these and turned to meaningless talk. "They want to be teachers of the law." These folks want to be teachers of the law but they do not know what they're talking about or what they so confidently affirm. Have you ever noticed that some people can get up and quote Scriptures, literature, and history, and try to put thoughts together and end up saying two plus two equals five? They are just reading between the lines. II Corinthians 4:2 (NIV), "Rather, we have renounced secret and shameful ways; we do not use deception, nor do we distort the Word of God. On the contrary, by setting forth the truth plainly we commend ourselves to every man's conscience in the sight of God." But, oh, how easy it is for some preachers to get a following of people who want to run after such novel ideas rather than what they hear from the plain ole preacher and the plain ole Bible. And people go running around from conference to conference to hear these special speakers who come up with these things that they find, so to speak, in Scripture. And they find symbols of what this number means and what this color means, that only they understand and dig out somewhere. But Scripture does not say what they are saying; they are making it up, but they really believe it. And some people just drool after such erroneous teachings that are just hair brained ideas that somebody has.

I will never forget what Adrian Rogers told the lady who came up to him one time. She looked at him with a wild look in her eye and said,

111

"Brother Adrian, I have a question for you." He said, "Yes?" And she said, "I would like to know, what is the meaning of that white horse in Revelation?" And he looked at her very seriously and said, "Ma'am, I believe that white horse is a. . . white horse." And you know folks, that is just about how it is. If we are not careful, we get out of the Bible what we put into it: speculation, guesswork, genealogies, myths, fables, tales, and humanly concocted ideas. I don't know about you, but I want to hear the truth of God; and I want to hear the Word of God! When the Word of God is expounded, that doesn't mean that we try to find things that it doesn't say. It means to explain the real meaning of what it is saying— and not trying to make it say what it is not saying, when it is not even in the text. You can't get anything better than plain ole Jesus!

19.

Pastor, Where Is Your Glow?

Moses' face glowed when he came off Mount Sinai, being in the presence of God. Exodus 34:29-31(NIV) "When Moses came down from Mount Sinai with the two tablets of the Testimony in his hands, he was not aware that his face was radiant because he had spoken with the LORD. When Aaron and all the Israelites saw Moses, his face was radiant, and they were afraid to come near him. But Moses called to them and talked with them." The point is that being in the presence of God can warm your heart. And it is evident in your life when you have been in the presence of God.

Nowadays when we are in the presence of God our face may not literally, physically glow, but the Bible does say that we are light. Matthew 5:14 (NIV) tells us this, "You are the light of the world, a city on a hill cannot be hidden. Neither do people light a lamp and put it under a bowl. Instead they put it on its stand, and it gives light to everyone in the house. In the same way, let your light shine before men, that they may see your good deeds and praise your Father in heaven." When Jesus is in our heart the light is in us, and we become a new man in Christ. So therefore, we also are light. The question is, "Pastor, are you glowing? Do people see you as the light of Christ shining forth in your words and deeds? Are your attitudes expressed on your face, or is your disposition sour, gloomy, and dark?"

Indeed, if you have been in the presence of God like Moses was and in your prayer closet and time with the Lord, you should be glowing. So, is there a glow about you that attracts people to the light of the Lord Jesus Christ? John 5:35 speaks of this where Jesus says about John the Baptist, "John was a lamp that burned and gave light, and you chose for a time to enjoy his light." He is talking about how people came to the light that they saw in John the Baptist—that attracted people. So pastor, are you sour, are you negative, or are you the type of person who walks in the light and enjoys the light of Christ? What are you reflecting? What comes out of your life that makes people want to be around you? Are you glowing? It reminds me in Revelation where the church at Laodicea wasn't cold and it wasn't hot but was lukewarm. They were supposed to be on fire for the Lord.

113

Romans 12:11 (NIV) "Never be lacking in zeal, but keep your spiritual fervor, serving the Lord." The word "fervor" in Strong's concordance is defined as: to be hot (boil, of liquids; or glow, of solids), i.e. be fervid or earnest, be fervent. The noun form means zeal, ardor. We are supposed to burn with zeal for the Lord Jesus, to be in love with Him and with other people. And that glow, that fire, that burning, that hotness should be evident in our lives. That has to do with our personal walk with Christ on a daily basis, our relationship to Him, our fellowship with Him, walking in communion with Him, and allowing the light that is within us to shine forth allowing the Christ within us to be manifested forth so that other people would see Jesus in us and see that light in us. Keep glowing for Jesus!

A similar attribute of glowing is courage. Acts 4:13 (NIV) "When they saw the courage of Peter and John and realized that they were unschooled, ordinary men, they were astonished and they took note that these men had been with Jesus." We see here that Peter and John had been put in jail for preaching the gospel, and they were being interviewed. Even during the interview they continued to boldly proclaim Christ, and He was very evident in their lives. The Bible says they saw the courage of Peter and John— just like Moses, being in the presence of God and his face glowed. Peter and John were also in the presence of Jesus in their daily lives walking and experiencing His presence; thus, their courage was manifested and people could see their courage that they had.

So the question is, "Pastor, where is your courage?" Is your courage evident or are you manifesting fear, worry, doubt, and anxiety in your life? Or when people see you, talk to you, observe you, do they see courage? Are you trusting in God so that you are not afraid of following God, and obeying Him, and helping the church move into the direction that it needs to go? As you deal with people and events and circumstances (the good, the bad, and the ugly), what comes forth out of your life that people see? Do they see you glowing with courage? My prayer for you is that (like Peter and John) people see courage in you. And my prayer for myself is that I would maintain my courage and it would be manifested so that people could see that in my life.

The other half of that verse of Acts 4:13 says, "They took note that these men had been with Jesus." You know, it is evident whether or not you've been hanging around with Jesus. It is one thing to have Jesus in

114

your heart as your Savior; it's another thing to hang out with Him on a daily basis. It is noticeable when you maintain your focus on Him, and you maintain your surrender to Him. So if you're not red-hot, pastor, don't expect the congregation to be red-hot. You might as well expect lukewarmness from the congregation if you're not red-hot. You need to be full of courage. Basically, it means to be filled with the Spirit.

Previously in Acts 4, Peter was filled with the Spirit when he spoke those courageous words to those who were talking to him. It's very important what you display—and it is not a show or phony emotion. It is the real thing being manifested in your life—your red-hot fearless relationship with the Lord Jesus Christ that people can actually see in your life. Glow with the Flow!

20.

Lessons from Hosea

In the book of Hosea we can find some pointers how God used Hosea to speak to the people as He talked about the priests and the prophets. Hosea 4:8 (NIV) "They feed on the sins of my people and relish their wickedness." The priests were making themselves fat cats off of the people by taking advantage of them and by feeding on their sins. A similar situation is found in I Samuel 2 when the Israelites would offer their sacrifices, but the sons of Eli would dip in and get the choicest parts of the sacrifices. In verse 29 God says, "Why do you scorn my sacrifice and offering that I prescribed for my dwelling? Why do you honor your sons more than me by fattening yourselves on the choicest parts of every offering made by my people Israel?" God says that the priest had scorned and even showed contempt towards the sacrifices and offerings the people were giving. I know that a pastor today is not a priest in the sense of the Old Testament term, but priests were spiritual leaders. Priests stood before God for man; and before man for God.

Pastors are spiritual leaders, and they have to be careful and very cautious that they don't feed on the sins of the people or seek to pad their pockets off of the congregation or flock that they are ministering to. In other words, there is a saying, "Dangle a carrot in front of a horse and he will pull the wagon." So pastor, what carrot is being dangled in front of you? (a nice salary, a raise, retirement, parsonage, compliments, perks.) Do you profit from members' sins rather than helping cure them? Do you compromise the message and/or your leadership? God is looking for both preachers and pastors who won't chase after carrots. I'm not a dumb animal but I am a servant of the most high God. I can't be bought.

So pastor, preach the Word, the whole counsel of God like in Hosea 4:6, "My people are destroyed for lack of knowledge." God was talking about the Israelites. Their spiritual leaders had not been giving them the knowledge of God; therefore the people were being destroyed. Sometimes people in the church act ignorantly because they have not been properly taught the whole counsel of God. One purpose of this book is to point out God's knowledge to pastors, so pastors will not be destroyed (through sin, discouragement, or ignorance). In Matthew 12:17 (NIV) Jesus said to the Pharisees, "If you had known what these words mean, 'I desire mercy, and not sacrifice,' you would not have condemned the innocent." Here the Lord Jesus was letting the Pharisees know that sometimes they did not have the right teachings or lifestyle (especially in dealing with others) because they lacked the knowledge of what the Scripture really meant. Therefore, this lack of knowledge led to their condemning of other people in an unnecessary way.

Another lesson in Hosea is found in 6:5 where it says, "Therefore I cut you in pieces with my prophets, I killed you with the words of my mouth." The word "cut" means "hued" like hued from a log and it is for the purpose of shaping. God used the prophets in Israel to help shape the people. So we see that part of a pastor's job is like being a modern-day prophet. The word "prophet" in the New Testament is generically defined as to "speak forth the word of God," not just someone who foretells the future. So a preacher, a pastor, is to speak forth the Word of God, or that is, to prophesy. We can learn from those prophets. One of the ways God used those Old Testament prophets was to "cut" the people in pieces. The Word of God cuts. It's quick and powerful, sharp as a two-edged sword (Hebrews 4:12). What was cutting them? Refer back to Hosea 5:15, "Then I will go back to my place until they admit their guilt." So the pastor preaches the Word of God, and sometimes people feel guilty. With guilt you can do one of two things. You can either repent of what you are being convicted of, and get your heart right with God and continue to grow. Or if you choose not to repent, then you want to reject the messenger (which would be the preacher) and just continue on your merry, sinful way. The Israelites chose to do the latter.

Hosea 8:8 "Israel is swallowed up; now she is among the nations like a worthless thing." United States churches' testimony and influence, I think, are described here, including a pastor's influence that has let others in the church (boards, or committees or whoever) or his own ambitions swallow him. It says Israel is swallowed up. However, the thought of a group of people in the church (or even outside the church) trying to swallow up the pastor, the preacher, reminds me of a saying I heard an evangelist say, "If they try to swallow me, I'm going down sideways!"

Hosea 10:13 "But you have planted wickedness, you have reaped evil, you have eaten the fruit of deception. Because you have depended on your own strength and on your many warriors." God was telling the Israelites that they had been depending on their own resources and depending on others. The word here is, Pastor, don't depend on rich men. A church should not depend on those in it that are rich. In other words, the church should depend, by faith, upon God. Otherwise it would be too easy to let those in the church who are wealthy to have more influence in the direction of the church because of their wealth. Or it would be easy for a pastor to allow his own life to be influenced by wealthy men who want to get their way by trying to use their wealth to bribe the pastor.

Hosea 13:6 (NIV) "When I fed them, they were satisfied; when they were satisfied, they became proud; then they forgot me." It's easy to forget God and become complacent in our lives, and that's what happened to the Israelites. They had to depend on God as they were in the wilderness. But when God told them they were going up to the promised land, He gave them a warning and told them to be careful that when they got into the promised land they would have so much that they could forget about Him.

In other words, they could lose their sense of dependency upon Him. Churches can get this way. A church can start out with great acts of faith, great steps of faith from small beginnings. Then sometimes as a church grows and gets more things (a nice building, a nice program, a nice staff), it is easy to become complacent. Perhaps they think they don't have to depend upon God now as much as they used to earlier, when conditions were a little tougher for them. So be aware of that, Pastor, in the church's life as well as in your own life. But don't be surprised if as a church grows, it ends up losing its power even though it may be growing in number and in finances. It's possible to lose its original vision.

Hosea 10:12 (NIV) says, "Sow for yourselves righteousness, reap the fruit of unfailing love, and break up your unplowed ground; for it is time to seek the Lord, until He comes and showers righteousness on you." One of the purposes of having a revival meeting or a special conference in the church is to have a time to go deeper and with more intensity than you had been going. This is an illustration from farming that sometimes as ground lays fallow it can develop a hardpan underneath the surface. And every now and then the farmer needs to come in with a bigger plow that plows deeper. Otherwise, as the rain water comes it gets no further down into the soil because there is a hardpan underneath.

Sometimes in Christians' hearts they can develop a hardpan. Then the church needs a revival meeting or special meetings using guest speakers (especially certain gifted men according to the New Testament like evangelists and prophets), who can be a penetrating plow to dig a little deeper furrow and break up the fallow ground in people's hearts. Of course, that may happen to us personally as pastors, and we need to be careful that we don't develop that hardpan in our own hearts, but have a tender heart toward the Lord.

Another lesson from the book of Hosea that illustrates the pastorate is in chapter 11:1-4 (NIV). "When Israel was a child, I loved him, and out of Egypt I called my son. But the more I called Israel, the further they went from me. They sacrificed to the Baals and they burned incense to images. It was I who taught Ephraim to walk, taking them by the arms; but they did not realize it was I who healed them. I led them with cords of human kindness, with ties of love; I lifted the yoke from their neck and bent down to feed them." This illustrates how the pastor loves a church just as God loved Israel when Israel was a child. God was saying, "I loved them but it seemed like the more I loved them, the more I called them, the further they went from me." That happens sometimes in the church where the pastor pours himself into the church, sacrificing for the church, for the people, for the ministry. And he pours out his love to them, but sometimes the more he pours out his love, the further they seem to stray away from him and from the Lord.

I have a dear friend who was married and had a baby girl. It turned out that the wife was not as she should be, and so there was a divorce. My friend ended up with custody of the baby girl. He poured out his life and his love, and sacrificed for this girl. As she grew she sometimes visited her birth mother. She would come home different and a little harder towards my friend, her dad. But it seemed that the more he loved her and helped her, the further she went from him. God taught Ephraim to walk, as my friend taught his child to walk, taking her by the arms. And even though he invested much of his life into her raising, as she got older she turned against him. She turned to the mother who had not been at all the mother she should have been to start with to this child. Sometimes that is the way it is with the pastor and the church. The pastor works for the church's good, but sometimes a church turns against the very one, the very good pastor, who is trying to help them and nurture them. Church people, Christians and so-called Christians can turn away from the reaching out of a loving pastor and turn their affection, their care, and their obedience to someone else. Here it says "I was called out of Egypt. Out of Egypt I called my son." Egypt also represents the world system. God calls the pastor out of the world system.

It also says that "it was I who taught Ephraim to walk." God teaches a pastor to walk. This is very important (being compared to teaching a child to walk). For instance, the pastor learns to walk—not merely by seminary classes, Bible school classes, reading good books, religious books, or by religious activities. So Pastor, learning how to walk is from God Himself! You can learn a lot of other things out there, and then God can use tools to help you. But it is God who teaches you to walk, just like a parent teaches a little child to walk. It went ahead to say that Israel made sacrifices to Baal in spite of the fact that God so loved them. He should have been the only God that they would sacrifice to. My prayer is, "Oh, God, help me never to offer sacrifices to Baal. May I only look to you for instruction and guidance in my life, and be submissive only to you and not to Baal or to a world system."

21.

Lessons from Amos

Amos 3:7 (NIV) "Surely the Sovereign LORD does nothing without revealing His plan to His servants the prophets." God reveals His plan for the church to the pastor. This, of course, in the Old Testament was applied to the prophets over the nation of Israel. It could include prophecy concerning them and the world situation, but I'm using this as an illustration for today in the church—that God will reveal His plan to the pastors of the church. So that we will know what direction God wants us to go. We do need to know God's plan. If we don't know, we need to get on our knees and search out His Word until we do know what His plan is at any given time in any given situation—so that then we can plan the work and then work the plan.

Amos 3:12 (NIV) "This is what the LORD says: 'As a shepherd saves from the lion's mouth only two leg bones or a piece of an ear, so will the Israelites be saved." Just as King David, when he was a shepherd boy would be watching the sheep and would see a lion attack a sheep, would run over to rescue the sheep and sometimes literally pull the sheep out the lion's mouth. A good pastor today, a good shepherd today, will be observant and watchful to see if one of the sheep is being taken in by Satan. And rather than just give up on the sheep, the pastor should run to where the sheep is that is suffering, that is hurting, that is being taken in by the enemy. The pastor should seek to pull that church member from the lion's mouth, from the devil's mouth, even if the only thing sticking out of his mouth is a leg. In other words, the pastor should do all that he can do to rescue the sheep— not just say what a stupid sheep it is.

Amos 2:4 (NIV) "This is what the LORD says: "For three sins of Judah, even for four, I will not turn back my wrath. Because they have rejected the law of the LORD and have not kept his decrees, because they have been led astray by false gods, the gods their ancestors followed." Some of the false gods that they followed were lies of Satan, lies of the enemy. Of course, the only weapons the devil has today are lies, as far as it concerns Christians. The Israelites are compared to dumb sheep, and they have been led astray by dumb sheep. The Bible also compares us to sheep. It doesn't compare us to cows, which can mostly take care of themselves. But a sheep is so defenseless, and sometimes the sheep doesn't have much sense. That is why it needs a shepherd. And that's why those lies need to be exposed. So the pastor needs to expose those lies and also share the truth of God and urge the people to follow the truth of God as opposed to the lies of Satan—so the sheep and his church will not be led astray in any way.

Amos 6:1(NIV) "Woe to you who are complacent in Zion, and to you who feel secure on Mount Samaria, you notable men of the foremost nation, to whom the people of Israel come!" Israel had gotten complacent. They had gotten at ease in Zion. So one of the pastor's jobs is to comfort the afflicted and to afflict the comfortable! Sometimes a Christian can lose his first love and become lukewarm. He can also become complacent today in the church. So the pastor should attack that complacency and stir up the people to get off the fence and serve the Lord with a fervent heart.

Amos 4:12 (NIV) "Therefore this is what I will do to you, Israel, and because I will do this to you, prepare to meet your God, O Israel." What does that mean? How do you prepare to meet God? 5:4 tell us, "This is what the LORD says to the house of Israel: 'Seek me and live, do not seek Bethel, do not go to Gilgal, do not journey to Beersheba.'" The pastor should teach the people how to seek God, that they should seek God. How to prepare to meet God is to seek God. Much teaching should be given on seeking God, the importance of seeking God and what it means to seek God. This would involve getting into the Word, studying the Word, meditating upon the Word, applying the Word, living by the Word and submission to Christ. As you seek God, you are allowing the Lord Jesus to live his life through you—not only in you but through you. You can either seek your viewpoints and your ways of doing things or seek Him and His ways.

Jeremiah 29:13 (NIV) "You will seek me and find me when you seek me with all your heart." So it's very important for the pastor to seek God! You are to seek God and live. You are to set the example of what it means to seek God. As the people see you seeking God, and as you explain what that is out of your own personal testimony of your own life, this will help them know how they also can seek God and then follow your example of seeking God.

22

The Importance of Friends in the Church

It is rewarding to revisit former church members. Some pastors make it a policy to never go back to a church where he used to pastor. That's his privilege. However, I have found it very rewarding to go back, not in any way to interfere with what a new pastor is doing. But if it was a good experience, and if you made friends at that church, a friend is a friend for life. It's okay to go back and visit them and is also encouraging to know that I had been a vital part of their lives; in other words, to go back years later and see how they have grown in the Lord and/or to see how they have developed in their ministry with the Lord.

I remember visiting a former church member a while back, and we reflected on how we first met. He showed up in my office but I really didn't know him. However, he had attended a wedding that I had recently performed, and I was probably the only preacher he had any contact with. He came in and sat down in my office and said, "I wonder if God could help me? I have been heavily into drugs and into Satan worship, and my life is a mess, and I want to get out of this lifestyle. Can God help me?" I assured him that he had come to the right place and, of course, God could help him. I talked with him, and shared with him, and prayed with him. He prayed, and he surrendered his life to Christ and he renounced his former lifestyle. One thing about him: because of his use of drugs he had become, according to the doctors, mentally disabled and was not able to work. My way of saying it is: his brain was probably fried from drugs. And so he was drawing a disability check each month from the government, and he didn't have a job.

As we continued to share and he continued to grow in the Lord, he recognized his need to work; and God continued to heal his mind and his soul. After a period of time he was able to start working and got a job in one of the biggest hospitals in the St. Louis area as a maintenance man. Some months later I walked into that hospital. On the bulletin board as you walk in, there are plaques of the 'Employee of the Year,' and I looked and his name was there! He had worked his way up to being Employee of the Year. He had gotten totally off of his disability checks because, of course, he was no longer disabled. God had totally restored his mind as well as his heart! What a beautiful and wonderful success story. He became a great worker in our church. Again, I met him years later. By this time his family had moved to another community. And in this community he and his family had found a new church home. They had started a children's program during the week. And they were very vital workers in the church. So it was very encouraging to me to see the fruit that had come out from some of the labor that I had put into the ministry while at that previous church.

Along the theme of visiting with former church members, I remember in the first church I ever pastored in Texas there was a man named Alfred. He was one of the deacons, a godly man, and a fine example of what a deacon should be. He and his wife were very supportive of me and my family, and we became good friends. I was only in that church for about a year. After graduating from seminary I moved on to other places. Years later when I turned 60 years old, my wife threw a surprise birthday party for me in Kansas where we lived. I was very pleasantly surprised to see Alfred show up. He had driven all the way from Texas to come and see me!

So there are a lot of benefits to maintaining friendships that you make in your ministry and in your churches where you may pastor. I don't know whoever came up with the idea that somehow that was not ethical. It's very Scriptural. The apostle Paul, more than once, sometimes would go back to a former church that he had pastored. There are many, many names that he mentions that he would visit and revisit from previous ministries, maintaining contacts over the years. If you really love someone, that love doesn't stop just because you get separated by miles.

So friendship is a great gift from God, and it is a great perk of being a pastor. Those friendships can continue to grow even though many miles and years may separate you. But it is indeed a blessing that we need to avail ourselves of. It is one of the positives of being a pastor and meeting so many wonderful people.

23

Random Thoughts

"It is not for kings, Lemuel—not for kings to drink wine, not for rulers to crave beer." (Proverbs 31:4).   Sometimes in the ministry we are tempted to just coast and think, "Well, I'm getting by in my life. I'm not committing any grave sins." But sometimes if you want to see more power operate in your life as a pastor and minister, you have a higher standard to live up to than the common person in the pew. So you have a choice: if you want to indulge yourself in some things that may be questionable or that you can justify or rationalize why it is okay, maybe it is okay for the average Christian. But the Bible says more is required of teachers. So if you want to live like a king, if you want the authority of a king, if you want a ministry that is above average, if you want to see God's power working in and through you in a supernatural way, then you need to consider your lifestyle and the things that you may think are okay for you to indulge in. Early in my ministry God allowed me to discover a magnificent essay which expresses this principle:

"Others May. . . You Cannot"
"If God has called you to be really like Jesus He will draw you into a life of crucifixion and humility, and put upon you such demands of obedience, that you will not be able to follow other people, or measure yourself by other Christians, and in many ways He will seem to let other people do things which He will not let you do.

Other Christians and ministers, who seem very religious and useful, may push themselves, pull wires, and work schemes to carry out their plans, but you cannot do it, and if you attempt it, you will meet with such failure and rebuke from the Lord as to make you sorely penitent.

Others may boast of themselves, of their work, of their successes, of their writings, but the Holy Spirit will not allow you to do any such thing, and if you begin it, He will lead you into some deep mortification that will make you despise yourself and all your good works.

Others may be allowed to succeed in making money, or may have a legacy left to them, but it is likely God will keep you poor, because He wants you to have something far better than gold, namely, a helpless dependence upon Him, that He may have the privilege of supplying your needs day by day out of an unseen treasury.

The Lord may let others be honored and put forward, and keep you hidden in obscurity, because He wants to produce some choice fragrant fruit for His coming glory, which can only be produced in the shade. He may let others be great, but keep you small. He may let others do a work for Him and get the credit for it, but He will make you work and toil on without knowing how much you are doing; and then to make your work still more precious He may let others get credit for the work which you have done, and thus **make your reward ten times greater when Jesus comes**.

The Holy Spirit will put a strict watch over you, with a jealous love, and will rebuke you for little words and feelings or for wasting your time, which other Christians never feel distressed over. So make up your mind that God is an infinite Sovereign, and has a right to do as He pleases with His own. He may not explain to you a thousand things which puzzle your reason in his dealings with you, but if you absolutely sell yourself to be His love slave, He will wrap you up in a jealous love, and bestow upon you many blessings which come only to those who are in the inner circle.

Settle it forever, then, that you are to **deal directly with the Holy Spirit,** and that He is to have the privilege of tying your tongue, or chaining your hand, or closing your eyes, in ways that He does not seem to use with others. Now, when you are so possessed with the living God that you are, in your secret heart, pleased and delighted over this **peculiar, personal, private, jealous guardianship and management of the Holy Spirit over your life,** you will have found the vestibule of Heaven." -- Author Unknown

Wow! I hope that blessed you like it did me. Many times during my ministry I have had to go back and reread this article and be reminded of what Jesus said in Mark 9:35(NIV) "If anyone wants to be first, he must be the very last, and the servant of all." As we are living in the last days, we pastors need not waste our time trying to be like other pastors or religious leaders, or for that matter, the leaders of any organization. True pastoring requires a servant's heart. This attitude of servant hood brings us into a closer identification with Jesus, the greatest servant of all. Romans 8:35-37 (NIV) "Who shall separate us from the love of Christ?

Shall tribulation or hardship or persecution or famine or nakedness or danger or sword? As it is written; 'For your sake we face death all day long; we are considered as sheep to be slaughtered.' No, in all these things we're more than conquerors through Him who loved us."

Is That a Hill Worth Dying On?

There is a saying "some hills aren't worth dying on". What this means is that in the military sometimes battles are fought for a certain hill, because it would be a good position—perhaps to put an extra air strip on, or it's a good defensive piece of ground. And men die to conquer that hill. An acquaintance of mine was a Marine in World War II. His company was ordered to conquer a certain hill occupied by the Japanese on an island in the Pacific. There was fierce fighting and many men lost their lives on that hill. The Marines won the fight and took over that hill. A few days later orders came from headquarters to leave that island because it had been determined that that hill was not so strategic after all. My acquaintance and his buddies said, "What a waste of lives; that hill wasn't worth dying on!" And in the church, battles are fought between people, staff, committees, and organizations. The pastor must be careful to consider, "Is that a hill worth dying on?" Just how important is it to win that particular battle? Some issues are better left alone.

I Don't Have a Dog in That Fight

Another phrase I like is, "I don't have a dog in that fight." Various church members may get crossways with each other, family members, or people in the community. And you must consider whether you have a dog in that fight. Is it really all that important for you to get involved? Because if it is not your dog (your concern) in the fight, but it's just two other people and their dogs that are in their fight, maybe you better keep your nose out of their business! Proverbs 26:17 "He that passeth by, and meddleth with strife belonging not to him, is like one that taketh a dog by the ears."

Sometimes it's just better to say to yourself (when you get to thinking that you have got to go and solve all the world's problems and settle everything for everybody) maybe you don't have a dog in that fight, and that's not a hill worth dying on. If you go and interfere, you can get yourself into trouble, or you could actually waste your time. So the pastor must consider when there is a conflict of any kind that's going on between people in the church or in the community, what is the pastor's role?

127

The Full Meal Deal

When we get saved we get the full meal deal. It's like going into a restaurant that offers a full meal deal such as a hamburger, fries, and a coke, and you get all of that for the price of one meal. Most Christians don't realize that when they got saved they got a full meal deal! They don't realize all they received with their salvation. Many Christians think that all they got was a ticket to Heaven. They don't realize all the abundant life, victorious life, the blessings, the power, and authority they got when they received Christ as Savior. So one of the roles of the pastor is to teach the folks what all they received when they got saved.

Out on a Limb?

Answering the call or obeying God may seem reckless to some. In other words, as people look at how we end up obeying the Lord and walking with Him, to the world it may seem foolish or reckless. But naïve faith is so beautiful, God finds it irresistible. There's something about a naïve faith that seems to place one in God's protective custody—mentally, emotionally, spiritually and even sometimes physically. So you have to be careful when you are responding to a call, because it would be easy for man, (especially for people who maybe aren't walking in the Spirit) to try and discourage you or make you think you're doing something foolish or reckless.

Satan's Trap for Pastors

Satan doesn't care how he ruins our ministry, just as long as he does. Satan can tempt with money, sex, power, pride, discouragement. Pride accompanied by a harsh, aloof, dictator spirit disqualifies you as a spiritual leader. Rather be kind, gentle, and humble, which is the opposite of pride. No man can give the impression that he is clever and that Christ is mighty to save. I Corinthians 2:1-5 "And I, brethren, when I came to you, came not with excellency of speech or of wisdom, declaring unto you the testimony of God. For I determined not to know anything among you, save Jesus Christ, and Him crucified. And I was with you in weakness, and in fear, and in much trembling. And my speech and my preaching were not with enticing words of man's wisdom, but in demonstration of the Spirit and of power: That your faith should not stand in the wisdom of men, but in the power of God." It is not our cleverness that people admire, but it is the power of God working in us! Matthew 20:27-28 "And whosoever will be chief among you, let him be your servant; Even as the

Son of man came not to be ministered unto, but to minister and to give His life a ransom for many."

Jeremiah Describes a Pastor

In Jeremiah we find some words that describe what a prophet does. Of course, the pastor does play the role of prophet in the sense that he's a preacher speaking forth the Word of God. The pastor is a watchman found in Jeremiah 6:17. The pastor is a tester of metals, 6:27. Words are a fire, 5:14. The pastor is an announcer, a proclaimer in 5:20. He is an observer in 5:1. He is also called a shepherd in Jeremiah.

Better Before Bigger

T.D. Jakes' prayer was not "God, make me bigger", but "make me better". Jakes said, "If the church gets better it will get bigger." God wants to build a pastor—not only a church. If the church builds up quicker and bigger than the pastor, then he becomes a poor leader and the church suffers. "Blessed are they which do hunger and thirst after righteousness." (Matthew 5:6). The word 'hunger' involves the idea of painful, like hunger pangs, and it involves the word "desperate." So Pastor, I encourage you to be hungry and desperate and to have hunger pains—hungering after righteousness in the Lord as opposed to hungering after the things of this world!

Can You Play a Trumpet?

Joel 2:1 (NIV) "Blow the trumpet in Zion; sound the alarm on my holy hill. Let all who live in the land tremble, for the day of the LORD is coming. It is close at hand." Here he was told to blow the trumpet in Zion. That could be a good illustration today of the pastor blowing the trumpet in the church and sounding the alarm because the day of the Lord is coming. The Lord is close at hand; in other words, Jesus' coming is very close. And the pastor should be teaching the church to have a sense of expectancy and living their life with a sense that Jesus could come back at any moment! So part of the pastor's role is to be a trumpet blower.

Can Doing Good Things Be Disobedience?

Even while I am trying to write this book, I have noticed a principle that as God is leading me to write this book, sometimes I have done other things: nice things, good things, pastoral things, ministering to people, visiting people, and preparing sermons. I tend, in my approach to ministry, to put people first and their needs. However, God has recently

129

laid it on my heart even more strongly to finish writing this book, because I kept allowing people ministry to take first place. I was not aware that I had a preconceived idea of what ministry to people meant. I had limited that idea that it had to be face-to-face to be ministry to people. But, duh, Roger, whoever reads this book is a people!

I don't know when Paul had the time in his busy ministry to write his epistles, but I thank God he did! It certainly has blessed all us down through the ages. And so, dear reader, my hope and prayer is that you are being blessed by the reading of this book. Therefore, by my writing this book, prayerfully I am ministering to the needs of people. Just writing this book has taught me to not put God in a box as for what my perception of ministry is. I was neglecting writing this book; which means I actually being disobedient, and that didn't dawn on me until now as I am writing the book.

This reminds me of a story I heard the about parents who had gone to town, and they left their boy at home. His chore that day was to paint the wooden fence around the yard. When they came back later in the day, they noticed that the fence had not been painted. However, they noticed that the boy had painted the barn. The dad says, "Son, I thought I asked you to paint the fence." He said, "Well, I decided to paint the barn because it needed painted." The dad said, "That is true that the barn needed painted, but what I wanted you to do was paint the fence; so therefore, you have disobeyed me."

That applies to a lot of life as we think of ministry. There are 101 ways we can go in ministry when we get up in the morning. They may all be good things to do. However, there's a certain fence God wants us to paint, but we are out there painting barns instead! So to even get this book finished I must concentrate on God's direction in my life to go ahead and write on this book, and finish this book, and paint the fence that <u>He</u> has assigned me. God only gives fruit or blesses, many times, that which He has instructed us to do. If I am not doing what He has instructed me to do, then I have noticed that I am not bearing the fruit in ministry that I've wanted to see; I mean seeing the result that only God can do (by the movement of His Spirit, of course, because I can't change people).

A Biblical example of this principle is found in Luke 10:38-42. Martha was reprimanded even though she was doing a "good thing."

It's almost like God has taken His hand off and said, "You can knock your brains out, Roger. You can work your fingers to the bone, and you can preach your heart out, minister until you drop, and you can preach to the needs of people but I'm not going to let you see much good from that." I guess one reason is so He will not be reinforcing my lack of fulfilling His priority in my life. He's made writing this book a priority. And I just haven't made it a priority. So He doesn't want to enable my wrong behavior, my lack of obedience in this. I don't get to pick and choose my ministry; it's God's kingdom, He's the king, He gives the orders!

Even so, I think there are times where there is some latitude, just like if a parent would say to a child, "You can go in the backyard and play." And then the child goes out in the backyard and plays. The child may choose to swing on the swing set, climb a tree, play in the sandbox, or whatever the child decides to do in the backyard within those parameters. The parent doesn't care at that moment, as long the child is in the backyard. The child has some choice there. However, if the parent were to say, "You can go into the backyard, but you cannot play in the sandbox," then it's obvious this is important to the parent, and the child has no other options, or else he would be choosing wrong behavior. Don't substitute the good for the best!

No Fruit?
Where there is no fruit, sometimes not only would God be trying to not reinforce wrong behavior on the part of the Christian, but also no fruit may exist because God is simply trying to guide you elsewhere in your line of ministry and saying what you're doing may be okay, but it's not the best. (See previous reference to Martha). There is a difference between the best and second-best! God is looking for His best will, which is His number one priority, to take place. Not to lose heart, sometimes we do get off track. That doesn't mean that God puts us on a shelf. It doesn't mean that absolutely nothing comes out of what we're trying to do. But I want to get the maximum! I want to see the most fruit for my life. And that only comes as we are operating within God's will—in His direction, walking in obedience to Him. The bottom line is as Jesus said, "I am the vine you are the branches, abide in me and you will bear much fruit." It's simply a matter of abiding in the vine. Abiding in the vine (besides what all else this means) means keeping our focus on Him and walking in obedience to what He is directing us to do in our personal lives and in our ministry.

131

You need to be so full of Christ that he sloshes out of you onto others. II Corinthians 2:15 "For we are unto God a sweet savor of Christ, in them that are saved, and in them that perish." In other words, you need to be so full of the Spirit that you're exuding with the attributes of Christ. And you're to be so full of Christ that He just spills over, and His attributes, His love, and His compassion, etc. spill out of you as you walk through life, and spill out over onto other people.

Get a Word from God

Do the world a favor and preach the Word. There's a difference between preaching about the Word and preaching the Word. You need Christ to get a word from God. In other words, to get a specific revelation or a rhema word. Jesus said to Peter "flesh and blood has not revealed this unto you but my Father which is in heaven." (Matthew 16:4). People don't come to church (or shouldn't come to church) to hear what man has to say. They need a word from God. And to get that word from God we must stay on our knees and in the Word ourselves and in an attitude of Christlikeness—walking with Him so that we can receive revelation so that the Word will be revealed (so we are not just parroting words off of paper). You know, the devil has memorized Scripture and the devil even quoted Scripture to Jesus. The devil knew the Word in his head but not in his heart. The Bible says, "Thy Word have I hid in mine heart that I might not sin against thee" (Psalm 119:11). So one of the pastor's (and preacher's) tasks is to get a word from God, then open your mouth and heart and let it fly!

My Wife

I made sure churches didn't expect any more of my wife than any other woman in the church. They are calling me to pastor, not her. She doesn't have to be on every committee. She would pray about how she wanted to be involved in the church and that was her business. Her main calling was to be my wife and a mother to our kids and whatever God called her to do.

A lot of churches don't realize the burden that is on a pastor's wife because she is the one that he would go home to from church, and he may feel like he has failed in his sermon, his efforts, or a committee meeting; and she can give him the assurance and encouragement that he needs. And she needs encouragement too, because the pastor leans on her a lot. I thank God that the churches that I have pastored have appreciated my wife. I am thankful for that and so is she.

132

God's Word is Exciting – Not Boring

Did you hear the story about the man who fell asleep during the sermon? The pastor looked at the man's wife and said, "Lady, please wake up your husband." She said, "You wake him up. You're the one who put him to sleep!"

Funerals

Memorialize the deceased. Comfort the grieving family. Uplift Christ. Give the plan of salvation, as some of the audience will never hear it anywhere else.

Weddings

Give the Biblical basis for marriage. Explain how marriage is a picture of Christ and the church. Share the basis of true love—Christ giving Himself on the cross. This is another good opportunity to share the plan of salvation.

Practical Advice

Always be on time. Be courteous. Exercise (I Corinthians 6:20— temple care). Eat healthy (Ephesians 5:29—nourish). Get a good night sleep. Take a day off every week. Use all your vacation days (not just for your sake, but for your family). Have a hobby (fish, golf, hunt, coin collecting, whatever). All work and no play make Jack a dull boy. Workaholism is a sin. Try to live debt free. Kiss your wife. Play with your kids, or grandkids.

Climb Down From Your Ivory Tower

Stay informed of the conditions where your flock lives. This includes what's going on in your local school (attend some of your students' ballgames or plays). Know what's going on in your town, county, state, country, etc. Sometimes hang out with the locals, like Jesus did. (Luke 19:7).

Don't Be a Loner

Seek fellowship with other pastors, and cooperate with them when you can. (Mark 9:38-40). Be part of the local ministerial alliance. Remember we are involved in the Kingdom, not just our local church.

Be Balanced

Feed the flock a balanced meal—for the young and old, for the mature and immature, for the downtrodden and the upbeat. Some sermons can talk about hell, some about heaven, some to convict of sin, some to encourage, some historical, some prophetical, some exegetical, some topical, some doctrinal, some tears, some laughter. (Acts 20:27). Teach that we have a miracle working God, but also teach that sometimes a miracle may not be His will. Read Ecclesiastes 3:1-8 and ask the Holy Spirit how this applies to your life and ministry.

Go On a Mission Trip

Get your church to send you to a mission field, so you can see missions firsthand. Take some members with you. This will deeply impact you all to better understand and support missions. Then your church can obey the Great Commission, "Go, and teach all nations" (Matthew 28:19), and fulfill Christ's last words, "Unto the uttermost part of the earth." (Acts 1:8).

Distinction Between the Universal Church and Local Church

Just because one has been saved and baptized by the Spirit into the Kingdom of God or universal church does not make him a member of a local church. Just because he attends a church doesn't make him a part of it. Just because a person is a friend of mine and comes to my house periodically does not mean he is a member of my family. Christ is the head of my home, but not just any Christian can come and claim rights to our possession or property or tell us how to use it.

The local church of our Lord is a fellowship, but more than a fellowship. The members of a civic club, such as Rotary or Kiwanis, may be compatible Christian people, working together on worthy goals, but they are not a New Testament Church.

The church in its universal sense is composed of all the redeemed people of God. It manifests or embodies itself in actual, visible local churches (bodies), e.g. seven churches in Asia (Revelation 2 – 3). "Let us not give up meeting together, as some are in the habit of doing, but let us encourage one another – all the more as you see the Day approaching." (Hebrews 10:25 NIV).

In almost every passage where ekklesia (church) is used, it refers to a visible, local, group of regenerated Christians organized or bound together to worship God, observe the ordinances, practice and promote the faith and doctrine of Christ, thus calling out and building up the "church of the firstborn" (Hebrews 12:23).

Each New Testament congregation made the major decisions about its life and work as led by the Bible and Holy Spirit. (Acts 13:1; 6:3; 14:23) The church is held responsible for the discipline of its members, not just everyone who attends (I Corinthians 5).

The universal church is built of living stones. It is made up of saints in heaven and saints on earth. And it is not identical with any one denominational body, or even all of them! Your local church is part of the worldwide Body of Christ!

To belong, be a member of, or join a local church you must first belong to the universal church (i.e. belong to Christ = be saved). Church members are not members of an organization or a building but are part of a Body—like arms and legs are members or part of a body. (I Corinthians 12:12).

Perhaps a better word than "join" a church would be to "commit" to a church. You let it be known that you want to walk in fellowship with a particular body of believers, putting yourself under that church's authority, and offering to use your gifts and talents to serve Christ in and through that church.

The church "members" should commit themselves to the new "member" to offer him love, fellowship, protection, and guidance, and opportunity to serve. This is a mutual bond and relationship is established, not just some piece of paper (or church membership roll.) I John 2:19 says, "They went out from us, but they were not of us; for if they had been of us, they would no doubt have continued with us; but went out, that they might be made manifest that they were not all of us."

The Pastor's Pay

I went to a pastor's meeting, where we would share about what had been going on in our lives over the past week. I shared about how "I have had a rough week at my church." One pastor responded, "Sounds like you've been earning your pay!"

"And when the Chief Shepherd appears, you will receive the crown of glory that will never fade away." (I Peter 5:4).

The pastor's retirement is out of this world!

24

SUMMARY OF THE PURPOSE OF THIS BOOK

I Timothy 1:18-19 (NIV) "Timothy, my son, I give you this instruction in keeping with the prophecies once made about you, so that by following them you may fight the good fight, holding on to faith and a good conscience." The idea here is related to training. A boxer trains to get himself ready for the fight. And the bottom line is pastors fight a spiritual battle. Of course all Christians do, but the pastor is at the forefront of the fight. The pastor is a fighter. He is fighting against false doctrine. He is fighting against the onslaught of Satan and demons of hell. He is fighting against false teachers, and he is fighting against those things harmful to his flock. He is fighting for the flock.

And so the pastor must not be a wimp, but he must be a fighter. He must stand his ground and stand for what is right and true. He is a soldier. In fact, II Timothy 2:3 says "thou therefore endure hardness as a good soldier of Jesus Christ." And so if a pastor doesn't stand and fight, if he's got thin skin (meaning he wears his feelings on his sleeves), if he is going to be offended and hurt and discouraged by the battle, then he needs to get right with God or drop out of the ministry, because in the ministry of Jesus Christ you are in the front line of battle.

There will be people turn against you, people who misunderstand you, and enemies who come against you, so just expect it. Paul said to Timothy, "I want to help prepare you to fight the good fight." And there are even fights in churches. You'll find that out in case you haven't been in churches very long! You will encounter some battles. Sometimes the battles come from without against the church, and sometimes the battle is within the church from members who come against the Kingdom of God advancing in the church, and come against the pastor. So the boxer, the fighter, needs to be trained to fight a good clean fight and not a carnal dirty fight like those coming against us. Jesus called us to fight the good fight. Jesus was a fighter, Jesus was a soldier, and Jesus was a good fighter. He didn't stoop to the level of the Pharisees and others who came against Him. He stood strong.

The purpose of this book is to help provide you, my pastor friend, with the tools, resources, ideas, insights, and encouragement (of whatever that

God may choose to use out of my life in some way) to alert you, to warn you, to prepare you for what you're going to face (speaking as one who has been there and done that). You will also encounter things that I've never encountered.

But at least those things I have encountered will, as Paul says, hopefully help you. "Who comforteth us in all our tribulation, that we may be able to comfort them who are in any trouble, by the comfort with which we ourselves are comforted of God." (II Corinthians 1:4). God can use some of those trials and tests (let's call them fights) to be able to help those who are going to be in the middle of similar trials, tests, and fights. And it's a fight you can win. Jesus already has won! He won at Calvary. We are winners in this fight. And understand as we fight we're not fighting against people, but we're fighting against principalities, powers, and rulers of darkness.

In a battle, who gets shot at the most? It is the soldier on the front line of battle. The pastor serves on the frontline. It should not surprise him when he is shot at. The pastor is a prime target of Satan. If you don't want to get shot at, get off the frontline, get out of the ministry. Jesus got shot at more than any soldier in history. He said, "If they persecuted me and the prophets, they will persecute you." (John 15:20). That's why Paul admonishes us to put on the full armor of God and to "stand." (Ephesians 6:11). Whining and griping, complaining, murmuring, feeling sorry for yourself, and blaming cantankerous church members is not "standing."

I found a great article describing the Christian as a soldier. The author is unknown. To help you not get battle fatigue, I share this article with you.

I Am a Soldier
"I am a soldier in the army of my God. The Lord Jesus Christ is my commanding officer. he holy Bible is my code of conduct. Faith, prayer and the Word are my weapons of warfare. I have been taught by the Holy Spirit, trained by experience, tried by adversity and tested by fire.

I am a volunteer in this army, and I am enlisted for eternity. I will either retire in this army at the rapture or die in this army. But I will not get out, sell out, be talked out or pushed out. I am faithful, reliable, capable, and dependable. If my God needs me, I am there. If He needs me in Sunday school, to teach the children, work with the youth, help adults or just sit and learn, He can use me because I am there!

I am a soldier, I am not a baby. I do not need to be pampered, pitied, primed up, pumped up, picked up or pepped up. I am a soldier. No one has to call me, remind me, write me, visit me, entice me or lure me. I am a soldier. I am not a wimp. I am in place, saluting my king, obeying His orders, praising His name and building His Kingdom! No one has to send me flowers, gifts, food, cards, or candy, or give me handouts. I do not need to be cuddled, cradled, cared for or catered to. I am committed. I cannot have my feelings hurt bad enough to turn me around. I cannot be discouraged enough to turn me aside. I cannot lose enough to cause me to quit.

When Jesus called me into this army, I had nothing. If I end up with nothing, I will still come out ahead. I will win. My God has and will continue to supply all of my needs. I am more than a conqueror. I will always triumph. I can do all things through Christ. The devil cannot defeat me. People cannot disillusion me. Whether cannot weary me. Sickness cannot stop me. Battles cannot beat me. Money cannot buy me. Governments cannot silence me, and hell cannot handle me. I am a soldier. Even death cannot destroy me. For when my Commander calls me from His battlefield, He will promote me to captain and then allow me to rule with Him. I am a soldier in the army, and I am marching claiming victory. I will not give up. I will not turn around. I am a soldier, marching Heaven bound.

Here I stand! Will you stand with me?"

25.

CONCLUSION

I conclude with an article someone gave me.

"Ministry Is:
Giving when you feel like keeping,
Praying for others when you need to be prayed for,
Feeding others when your own soul is hungry,
Living truth before people even when you can't see results,
Hurting with other people even when your own heart cannot be spoken,
Keeping your word even when it is not convenient,
It is being faithful when your flesh wants to run away."

Now, my pastor friend, get out there and let Jesus pastor through you!

18507295R00085

Made in the USA
Charleston, SC
07 April 2013